Agnes McAllister

A lone Woman in Africa

Six Years on the Kroo coast

Agnes McAllister

A lone Woman in Africa
Six Years on the Kroo coast

ISBN/EAN: 9783337119362

Printed in Europe, USA, Canada, Australia, Japan

Cover: Foto ©ninafisch / pixelio.de

More available books at **www.hansebooks.com**

A Lone Woman in Africa

SIX YEARS ON THE KROO COAST

BY

AGNES McALLISTER

MISSIONARY UNDER BISHOP WILLIAM TAYLOR

NEW YORK: EATON & MAINS
CINCINNATI: JENNINGS & PYE

Copyright by
HUNT & EATON,
1896.

Composition, electrotyping,
printing, and binding by
HUNT & EATON,
150 Fifth Ave., New York.

Miss Agnes McAllister is a christian heroine. She has been in charge of Garaway Mission Station on Kroo Coast, West Africa, for nearly eight years, and has made a success in all departments of our Mission work. She is at home now, on leave for a year, to tone up her overworked system, leaving her Mission in charge of her widowed Sister, Mrs Hunt, who is an efficient Missionary worker. Miss Agnes has written a book. It is full of graphic delineations of what she saw, suffered, heard and did in the babble of heathen life, and the ravages of war in which she took an active part as surgeon, nurse, and counselor.

150, Fifth Ave, N.Y.
August 14th 1895.

Wm Taylor.
B'p of Africa.

CONTENTS.

	PAGE
Introduction by Bishop William Taylor, . . .	5

CHAPTER I.
The Call to the Work, ... 11

CHAPTER II.
First Days in School, ... 28

CHAPTER III.
The War, ... 47

CHAPTER IV.
The End of the War, . . . 68

CHAPTER V.
Liberia—Its People, Languages, and Customs, . 85

CHAPTER VI.
Burying the Dead, ... 100

CHAPTER VII.
Native Theology and Morals, 116

CHAPTER VIII.
Incidents of Missionary Life, . 130

CHAPTER IX.
Visiting Neighboring Tribes, . . . 146

CHAPTER X.
In Journeyings Oft, ... 161

CONTENTS.

CHAPTER XI.
Ups and Downs, ... 179

CHAPTER XII.
Sasswood Palaver, ... 193

CHAPTER XIII.
The African Woman, . . . 210

CHAPTER XIV.
Farming.—African Curios, . . 233

CHAPTER XV.
House-building.—The Liquor Curse, . . 255

CHAPTER XVI.
A Revival, ... 270

ILLUSTRATIONS.

A Lone Woman in Africa, .	Frontispiece
Miss Agnes McAllister,	10
Garraway Mission House,	25
Men of Garraway,	33
A Trio of Witch Doctors, .	135
Children in an African Maize Field, .	216
Woman's Work in Africa, .	222
African Curios.—I,	240
African Curios.—II, .	248
West African House,	254

Miss Agnes McAllister,
OF GARRAWAY MISSION, LIBERIA.

A LONE WOMAN IN AFRICA.

CHAPTER I.

THE CALL TO THE WORK.

"There is Time enough yet."—Full Surrender.—A Voice out of the Night.—Off for Africa.—Monrovia.—Appointed to Garraway.—The first Sabbath.

WHILE attending Sabbath school in the old log schoolhouse in the neighborhood of my home, and listening to the sermons of the Methodist preachers, my heart was drawn to Jesus.

I well remember one Sabbath afternoon. The pastor, Rev. Mr. Swan, had announced that he would preach a sermon to the children. We sat in our classes with our teachers, the infant class in front. I was in the infant class, on the very front row; and I well remember that my feet did not touch the floor, for I was but seven years old. Miss Jennie Trever, our teacher, sat at the end of the same seat.

The preacher took for his text, "There is time enough yet." I have forgotten most that he said. But one story which he told I have never forgotten. He said that in a certain place a little boy and girl lived, with their mother, very near the sea; and one day the children begged of their mother to let them go down to the seaside to play. She let them go, but told them that they must not stay too long, as the tide would be coming in and they might be overtaken and drowned.

They went down to the beach, and found an old man sitting there. After they had played for a little while they said, "We must go home." But the old man said, "There is no hurry; there is plenty of time yet." So the children went back to play, but after a short time said again, "Well, it is time to go now." But the old man replied, "You need not hurry." "O," they said, "but our mother told us not to stay long because of the tide. We would better go now." "Yes," said the old man, "but there is plenty of time. There is time enough yet to have another good play." So the children went back to play, and the tide came rushing in, and they were both carried out to sea and drowned.

By this story the preacher showed what God meant when he said that now was the time to seek salvation. There was danger in delay. The devil, like the old man, was trying to persuade us to put off the decision; not by saying, "Don't go home," but just, "There is time enough yet." God had warned us that there was danger, and the Holy Spirit was drawing our hearts to himself; and it was for us to decide whether we would give him our hearts now, while we were young, or listen to the devil and be lost. That very afternoon I decided that I would give God my heart, for there was not "time enough yet." Then and there I yielded my heart to God, and from that time I sought to do God's will.

But it was not until I was fifteen that I joined the church, for I was surrounded by people that did not believe in children's being converted; and even at the age of fifteen I was considered too young to decide such a question. I had never heard much about holiness or a complete surrender to the will of God, and my highest aim was to be a good girl and keep the law of God, to trust in Jesus Christ for salvation, and to get to heaven. I was not very strong, and this world did not have much attraction for me; and even in my girlhood days I often wished and prayed God that I might not live long.

At nineteen years of age I attended a meeting where the minister took for his text, "Follow peace with all men, and holiness, without which no man shall see the Lord." I listened attentively to him as he made plain to us that the Holy Ghost was come to be our Comforter and Guide, and would abide with us if we would receive him. I learned that there was a new joy and a bright side to life that I had not yet seen; and I, among others, answered the invitation and went to the altar to surrender myself to God and receive all that he had for me. As we stood there while the minister talked to us before kneeling my strength gave way, and I sank to the floor and made a complete surrender, saying, "All I have I give to Thee." God accepted me, and the Holy Ghost so filled my heart that I knew I had stepped on new ground; and I rejoiced as never before.

I went on for some time rejoicing in the Lord, but always burdened for others. I had taken part in the public prayer meetings before this. But now I felt that I must speak to persons about their souls. I was not always kindly received in doing so. To satisfy my desire to do something for Christ I used to write short notes—any words that I thought might arrest the readers' attention and make them think—and then as I went along the street I would give them to those whom I met. I generally had a number ready on prayer meeting night, and as I went through the park I would drop them near the seats, to be picked up by the chance passer-by. I always folded these papers in the shape of notes, thinking so to induce the finder to examine them.

I began to think more seriously about the heathen, and to consider whether I might not be able to go and take the good news of salvation to those in darkness. But I was surprised at myself for letting such a thought ever enter my mind, for I, of all persons, seemed to be the most unlikely ever to go far from home. So I reasoned with myself and wondered and asked the Lord what he would have me do, feeling satisfied in myself that this was only a passing thought. But the burden grew heavier, and I became more and more concerned for others, until a Christian lady to whom I had confided my feelings said she thought it very possible that the Lord was calling me to the work, and if so he would make it plain in answer to prayer.

Although I had given myself to God entirely and thought I was ready to do anything for him, yet I found that a missionary's life, as I conceived it, was not pleasing to me. I hoped it might not be my lot, for I did not then look at it as a privilege to go to labor among the heathen. Nevertheless, I knew that the will of the Lord was the only safe guide for me, and I prayed that I might know with certainty what he would have me do, promising that if he would only make his will known beyond doubt I would go even to a foreign land.

After some days spent in prayer and serious thought the Lord declared his will. I was sitting in the house in the evening, just as it grew dark and quiet, when I thought I heard a step on the walk. Then there came a knock at the side door. I expected a friend to spend the evening with me. As I opened the door, however, and looked out into the dark no one was visible; but I heard a voice plainly say, "I want you to be a missionary." I recognized that this message was the answer to my prayer. I stood silent for a moment, then came in and closed the door. But I did not answer the call. I did not say, "Yes, I will go." When I went to dinner it seemed as if the food would choke me. I felt as if some person was following me, as I went about the house from room to room, saying, "Now what do you say? Will you go? Will you be a missionary?" The burden became so great that at last I sat down and cried, then bowed before my Saviour and said, "Yes, Lord. Grant me rest. I will go. I will do anything." So it was all settled. I know it was from the Lord. During all the time I have spent in Africa— six years and two months—I have never once doubted the fact that the Lord had called me to the work.

I wrote to my parents. Mother wrote back, "Well, I always thought you would do something of the kind." My friends were not surprised; and this made it much easier for me. The Lord gave me the privilege of spending some time in school in special preparation for the work, and I enjoyed some practical experience in city mission and revival work, which was one of the best things I could have done to prepare me to deal with the heathen. For human nature is the same in all lands, and many of the same excuses that we meet in the home land we meet in heathendom.

In reading the account of Bishop Taylor's work in Africa, my mind was drawn in that direction. The appeal to the Church, "Who will come over and help us among these poor dark sisters?" touched my heart, and I offered myself and was accepted. In 1888 I sailed for the west coast of Africa, and was stationed at Garraway, in Liberia, where I have been ever since. Many a day, when the work has been hard and everything has looked dark, I have thanked God that it was by no choice of mine that I was in this place, and that, no matter what had come or might come, I knew that I was called of God to the work. Thus I was never once discouraged. All the time I have praised God that, although the way was rough, yet it was bright to me.

Parting with home and friends, and all our familiar surroundings, to go to an unknown land is always hard. When I went out to Africa, it seemed a much greater undertaking than it does now. It was like burying me; for few thought that I would ever return. Nor had I any assurance myself that I should ever see the faces of my friends again. But the ways of the Lord are past finding out. His ways are not ours. I found kind friends on every hand to help me. As I knew that I was going to the most unlikely place in the world to procure articles for personal use, or for housekeeping, I supplied myself well with clothing. Many kind people who were interested in me gave me quilts and blankets and dishes as well as dried fruits and other things which they thought would be useful.

On December 13, 1888, we sailed—a party of fourteen—from New York harbor for Hamburg. We had a pleasant voyage, and entered the Elbe on the day before Christmas. We had to wait in Germany until the third of January for a steamer going down the African coast. On that day we set sail for the field of our labor. At first the weather was pleasant, and all went well; but when we came to the Bay of Biscay most of our party were down with seasickness. I was very sick for three days, and really felt as though I would as lief die as live. But we got through the bad water, and all were bright and happy again. We found it getting much warmer as we steamed southward.

When we came to Madeira, the young Portuguese boys came out to dive for money. They stayed around the ship all day, calling out to the passengers on deck, "A penny for a dive, sir!" "Sixpence for a dive, sir!" "One shilling, and I will go under the ship, sir!" As the passengers would throw the money into the water, they would jump in to get it, always coming up with the coin in their hand. But I shall never forget the feeling that came over me as I got the first sight of these people, who in some respects suggested heathendom.

We sailed to the coast of Africa, and cast anchor at Monrovia, about three miles out at sea. It is not safe to take the steamer near the beach, and there is no wharf; consequently, passengers and freight must go ashore in surfboats. When we approached the shore in these boats we had to anchor several yards out in the water, and a boat load of natives came alongside to take us to the beach. We stood up on the side of the boat, and they took us in their arms like babies, and set us down on the sand, making trips until all were landed.

We were met on the shore by one of the missionaries. As it was Sunday, and near the hour for service, we were all taken to the chapel, where we joined in worship with the crowd of natives that followed. They were very much pleased to see so many white people come to their country, and the little children would allow us to carry scarcely anything in our hands, they were so anxious to do something for us. African sights and sounds were every minute becoming more familiar; and from that day I felt that I really had reached the home of those whom I had come to help and lead to the Saviour. From the chapel we went to the mission house, where we had some "lime-ade"—made like lemonade, from a native fruit which is something like our lemon, and takes its place very well.

After a few hours on shore, which were a treat to us after the rolling of the ship for so long, we returned on board again. On the twenty-first of January we reached Cape Palmas, the end of our journey. We arrived in time to have gone ashore the same night, had the sea not been so rough. Some of the boats from the shore tried to reach us, but had to go back, as the sea was bad and the night dark. In the morning all was calm. We were called up before daylight, had a cup of coffee, and then started for the shore. It was about seven o'clock when we landed.

We were met by some of our missionaries who had been sent out the year before. Everything was strange enough to my eyes; but as Cape Palmas is one of the civilized towns of the Liberians, we did not see much of heathendom during our stay there. We saw the heathen as they came in to trade; but they lived in the surrounding country, and we saw little of their homes and manner of life. The supplies that we had brought with us to commence our work with had not come on the same steamer with us, and we were obliged to wait for them. Then Bishop Taylor was expected, and we had to await his arrival to receive our appointments. Several steamers passed, but he did not come. At last our agent started out up the coast to Sinoe, where the bishop was, to bring him down. After several days they returned together, and we all received our appointments. Our goods came, also, and at the end of three weeks we left for our several stations.

Sister Binkley and I were appointed to Garraway. We started for our new home on the sixteenth of February, 1889, Bishop Taylor and the mission carpenter and ourselves sitting on the top of the boxes and goods while we sailed up the coast twenty miles in an open surfboat. It was eight o'clock in the evening when we arrived. As we were carried ashore in the strong arms of the natives, a crowd of the people gathered around us, delighted to see so many white people, and to know that two women had come to stay among them. The station owned an iron building. This had been opened more than a year before by Rev. Mr. Gortner, his wife and two sons, and a Mrs. Meeker, who had come out as a teacher; but they had not been able to do any work among the people, being down with fever most of the time.

When the Gortners came the natives gave them a bullock and a sheep, for meat, in order to show their gratitude. The fever was less kind, and Brother Gortner, his wife and eldest son, and Sister Meeker were all confined to bed at the same time. Only the youngest son, about nine years of age, and an old Liberian woman were able to be about and do anything for the sick. Mrs. Meeker, who was well on in years and not very strong, was the first to die from the fever. It was in the afternoon that she left the work to be with her Lord; and in the evening of the same day Mr. Gortner also went to be with Jesus, "which is far better," leaving his wife and son too sick to help themselves or attend to burying their dead.

The Liberian woman took this opportunity to help herself to everything in the house that suited her fancy; and the two dead bodies lay there until the third day before anything was done toward burying them. Some sailors, hearing of the deaths at the mission, went up and made two coffins from the board partitions of the house and buried the bodies. Mrs. Gortner was too sick at the time to stand on her feet, and crept on her hands and knees to take a last look at her husband. On their return to Cape Palmas these Liberian sailors told what they had done, and our bishop being there, he went at once to Garraway and did what he could for the sick. Mrs. Gortner and her son recovered and returned to America, and the station was left in the care of an old native man and one of the Liberian women.

Soon after we reached Cape Palmas word was sent to Garraway that new missionaries had come, and that some person would soon be sent to take charge of the station. So a chicken was caught and tied, ready to be cooked for the first meal when the missionary should arrive. When we reached there that evening in February they killed and cooked the fowl, and prepared a dinner for us. We were all hungry, for we had been several hours on the water, had been seasick, and were quite ready to eat. The meal consisted of chicken soup, a native vegetable called *cassada*, some sea biscuits, and coffee. The soup smelt good, but, when we tasted it, it was so hot with the native red pepper that it brought the tears to our eyes, and we could not eat a mouthful.

A great crowd of the natives had followed us to the mission. Everything was new and strange to us, the mission house not less than the people. The house was built of galvanized iron, and was set up on posts six feet from the ground. As I entered it, I thought of a barn. The rough framework was all visible inside, for there was no ceiling. The partitions—what was left from the coffin making—were only hand-high, and the whole appearance of our future home was desolate enough. The crowd stayed till late; and as we were all very tired and needed sleep we told them that they had better go home. So they departed, and we found a place to sleep for the night. The missionaries that had been there before us had fixed up some beds, and we spread out our

Garraway Mission House.

blankets and lay down. All rested well, and in the morning the kings and chiefs came in to see us, and the carpenter put some chairs together that had been brought out in boxes, all ready to be fitted. After an early dinner the bishop left for the Cape, and we were alone. It was Saturday, and Miss Binkley and I set things in order.

The next day was Sunday. Although the people did not know the difference between that day and any other, many of them came to us out of curiosity, and we had a good service. Our first service was with the children, at half past nine in the morning. At eleven o'clock we had another service, with more of the old people present. At two we had another meeting, and still another at six. We had many of the same persons at the different services, as they stayed over from one service to the other. The day was very warm, and as we did not get any rest we were very tired at night. But we had told many people of Jesus, and retired feeling that the day had been well spent, and that the good seed had been planted that would yield fruit that should never pass away.

CHAPTER II.

FIRST DAYS IN SCHOOL.

A School among the Heathen.—Opening Day.—A Royal Beggar.—Teaching the Interpreter.—The Children of the Mission.—Clothes.—Farmwork.—Native Curiosity.—Left Alone.—"Zion Village."—The War.

ON Monday morning we promptly opened our school. A few minutes after six o'clock eager boys were waiting to have us teach them ; at half past eight we commenced with thirteen pupils and had school till ten. Five men sat and listened to the children and to our teaching. They said, "You teach book proper," which meant that they were satisfied that we knew how to teach their children. At two we had forty-five children and seven women present. Several of the women sewed some cloth very well, which showed us that they could sew if they cared to learn. At four a lot of new ones came in, and they had to have a lesson too. In the evening the old king brought all the old letters he had for me to read over to him. Some of them were five years old—letters that the coast traders had written to him.

The next day we had a crowded house.

After teaching the children until I was tired I told them they could go, for school was finished for them. But three of the larger ones succeeded in getting the rest outside and then came back, saying, "We did not have plenty lesson; we want to read more book." So I gave them slates and pencils and some letters to make, and they had a good lesson before they went away. Miss Binkley had a class of ten young men. After teaching them each a lesson separately, she told them to go home and come back the next day; but in the afternoon they were all back, bringing six more with them. So we had school again at two o'clock with fifty-one children and several women. These latter repeated their letters and printed them on their slates like the children, but wanted me to pay them for what they did! They brought their babies and were much pleased when we took them in our arms.

We were wondering what we should have for breakfast when one of the chiefs sent us a piece of deer meat, which was very acceptable to us. It was a small token of his feeling that he ought to do something for us because we were strangers who had come to do his people good. Frequently after this he would send us limes or bananas.

One of the king's sons came early one morning to beg us to give him some potatoes. I told him that it was a shame for him, a big, strong man, to ask us women to give him potatoes when he knew we were strangers and did not have plenty for ourselves. He did not understand me clearly; so I said, "We no got plenty chop [victuals]. One man in town send me chop this morning. You come here, you bring so so hand, no nothing live inside. You beg me for give you something for eat. What thing you live for do? You no got chop to eat. It be big shame for you to beg." He went home, and in an hour was back with a bowl of breadfruit, hot from the fire, and was pleased to see us sit down and eat it.

I took out with me from America two child's Bibles. Although none of the natives could read, all were interested in looking at the pictures and listening to the Bible stories. Every Sunday these books had to be gone over, and in this way several of the children learned many of the stories before they could read a word. All our readings had to be interpreted. As nobody in the tribe understood anything about the Bible the lessons had first to be taught to the interpreter; otherwise he would not have understood them, and the people would not have heard the truth. We never had a meeting without teaching the lesson to him thoroughly before we commenced the public service.

Many of our meetings were more like school than public meetings, for we found it necessary to ask questions and have the people answer them in order to fasten the truth in their minds. We had with us several of the bright-colored picture rolls prepared for Sunday schools and found it profitable to take the pictures for the subjects of our lessons. We pasted a number of them on the wall of the house, and as the people came in they would often look at them and explain them to each other. I had taken a number of photographs—for we had brought a camera—and was waiting for a chance to print some more. So I took a day for the work and printed several dozen. Some were good, but others were not, for the sea air had somewhat affected the plates, and I had no good place to print them.

It was one part of our argument with the people that they should give their children to the mission to be taught. But we had been at the station several weeks before we had any children given to us. All who had so far attended had come only for the day, going to their homes at night. But one day when we were visiting in town a devil-doctor called us and gave us his little boy, of seven years, saying, "Take this boy and teach him sense proper. You must give him chop and find a wife for him." A number of others intended to give their boys, but had been waiting to see who would be the first to send his son to be educated.

We took the devil-doctor's boy home with us, naked as he was given to us, thinking that, although he was not very promising, yet he might open the door for some that were. The first thing we did was to dress him. We made him for every day a little shirt and a breech-cloth such as the native men wear, and for Sunday a shirt waist, knee breeches, and a little white cap, all out of factory cotton. On Sunday we dressed him in his white suit and took him with us to town to service. How the people crowded round to see the little boy dressed like the white men! They were delighted. They had not supposed that one of their own children could look so well with clothes on. Few of them had ever seen a child dressed, and it was a revelation to them.

The result was that the next morning we got three more boys, and before the week was out we had nine. By Sunday we had them all dressed and took them to town in their fresh white cottons. The people were more than pleased. Some of them would put their

FROM "ILLUSTRATED AFRICA." Men of Garraway.

The devil-doctor in the fur cap was the father of the first boy who was given to the mission.

hands on the shoulders of the boys, call them by name, and say, "Is this really you? Why, how fine you are!" That day we went around to four towns and held services in them all, reaching home as it was getting dark. Soon we got more boys; but they did not all stay. Indeed, for some time we never took "our" children to town without bringing some of them home crying. They wanted to stay with their mothers; and their mothers often coaxed them away, wishing them to learn to catch fish so that they might have fish soup to drink. Some of the boys gave us trouble by running away; but after a while those that were not satisfied stayed away, and those that wanted to learn settled down to study, and we began to get things in order.

We took the early hours of the morning for work on the farm, had breakfast at ten o'clock, and school at eleven. After school the children had a lunch, generally of bananas or sugar cane, and then all were ready for work on the farm again. We had no farmer to take charge of the work, since we were living on as little money as possible; so I undertook to oversee the farm. It was my duty to go out as soon as the dew was off the grass and direct the boys. I took my sewing along and a chair and sat and sewed, while they cut the low bush, or hilled potatoes, or planted other vegetables. We cleared ground and planted five hundred coffee trees. We found it very difficult raising coffee, for the natives did not raise it, and few of them knew a coffee tree from a weed.

We tried to impress upon the people that they ought to wear clothes. As they knew little about sewing it fell to our lot to do a good deal of tailoring for them. They would bring us the cloth, and then work on the farm to pay for the making. This and our own sewing made our work very heavy, for we had little help and every duty required our attention.

In all our teaching we made it a special point to impress on the people the need of a Saviour and their dependence upon God. Some were very ready to receive the truth, and it made a great impression on them. One evening one of the young men came in in a great hurry on his way home from the farm to see me a few minutes. "Teacher," said he, "I dream all that you tell me about God last night. This morning I get up. I so well and happy." After I had played on the organ and sung to him for a while he exclaimed, "Now pray; I want to go home," and we all knelt in prayer.

Sometimes we had so many callers that it seemed as if all the people had taken a holiday and come to visit the mission. I had taken photographs of the native towns and a number of the people, and these pictures were a wonder to them. They were amazed to see themselves on paper, and used to say, " White man knows everything for true. He be all same as God. He fit to make man live."

The women who came to visit us were very curious. It was always a mystery to them what made the needle in our sewing machine go up and down without our touching it; and I often patched their towels or sewed a few stitches for them so that they might show their people in the interior what they had seen.

They were much amused with the organ, and often asked us to " make that box talk." While we were playing they would examine it all over to see where the sound was coming from. They never got tired of the organ, for they were very fond of music.

We had taken out a small cook stove, which was another source of wonderment. One would tell another about it, and they came for miles to see it. We had to open the door to let them see where the wood was put in, how the smoke went up the chimney, the holes where the pots were put on, and the oven where the bread was baked. They seemed to have an idea—until they learned better—that bread was all that white people ate.

Our bedroom we did not allow them to enter, and they thought that there must be something wonderful hidden away there that we did not want them to see. The king often asked why we would not allow them to go into that room. We must, he said, have some reason for it. We told him it was not the custom in our country. But he was never satisfied, and thought there was some secret reason for keeping the door always shut. So to satisfy him one day when he and a number of the other chiefs had come to see us, we took them in to examine the room. They were much pleased to be allowed to see for themselves, but, not finding anything of interest to them, they were a little disappointed that their hopes had not been realized.

But the women, who had never been away from home and had not seen as much as the men, were perfectly delighted with everything, and would clap their hands and snap their fingers, and use all kinds of expressions of surprise and joy. They had never dreamed that there were such wonderful things in the world as they saw in our house.

The people are much pleased to have white

people live among them. They consider it a benefit to their country. But some of them do not want to have this benefit mixed with too much religion. Our king—*Davis* is his English name—had been to England and knew that white people have much more of this world's goods than his people had, and he spoke English fairly well; but he never wanted to be talked with personally about salvation. We had never been able to induce him to stay for service. He always made some excuse. But one Sunday when he came up to see us Miss Binkley was ill and unable to be out of her room at service. When we knelt down to pray the king looked about for a place to get out of earshot, and went into the room where Miss Binkley was. But she, too, had knelt in prayer, and the king found her on her knees. He nudged her and told her to get up, but she paid no attention to him, and he had to wait and listen to our prayers for him.

After a few months Miss Binkley married one of our missionaries and went to live on the Cavalla River. I was left alone at Garraway. No heart which has not gone through the experience can imagine the feeling that comes over a Christian woman left alone among the heathen. God wonderfully sustains and comforts, and he upheld me; but I was human, and at times a realization of the great distance between me and any sympathizing heart and of the responsibility of the work would come over me with such force and weight that the only place where I could find relief would be at Jesus's feet. Many times as it grew dark I would go down the hillside to some quiet spot and there tell Jesus all the burden of my heart, have a good cry, and come back to take up the duties of mother and teacher to the children, of preacher and missionary to the people, of doctor to the sick, of superintendent of the work in general—besides teaching the children all that they learned out of school, as well as in school.

I think now of the days that are gone and the experiences that I passed through, when it seemed as if my frame could not endure another burden; and I realize how wonderfully my Saviour shared the burdens which I alone could not have borne. When I realize this I can but shed tears of joy and exclaim, " All praise to our victorious Lord ; his grace is sufficient." If I should never return to that dark land I would never cease to praise him for the grace with which he strengthened me in many a weary and lonely hour.

Our progress in teaching the children was necessarily slow. They could learn but little from their books until they could speak some English. Sometimes, to induce them to do their best, we offered prizes. We would review the English lessons they had had, and to the child who knew them best we gave a teaspoonful of sugar, a piece of bread, a card, or an extra hour for play. We did not have the trouble afterward that we had at first, for the older scholars helped us by teaching the younger ones.

Several of the young men in neighboring towns were anxious to learn; but they had other work to do, and the mission was too far away to allow them to come to school. So they moved away with their wives from the heathen influences in their old villages and built a new town near the mission, to which we gave the name of "Zion," meaning "the city of God." When our tribe settled on the coast they founded but one town, which they called Maquanka, meaning " we all sit down together."

Some time after this a part of them desired to move out and make a new town. The rest objected; but the discontented ones persisted, and built a village called Ballie, which in their language means "we beg you." After a while still another part of the old settlement became dissatisfied and though the people in the old town defied them to build a new town, they did so, and called it Hesseka, which is "we dare you." So it was quite in keeping with their customs for us to call our town Zion.

The men of Zion were very anxious to learn; but they had their families to care for, and could not be regular at school. They would come, however, whenever they had a little spare time. We always made it a point to pay special attention to them. They learned some things of great service to them and were very proud to be able to read and write and do some arithmetic. The women of Zion had not the same desire to learn. They knew no English, and it was much harder for them to learn, and they soon stopped trying.

We found it difficult to get the women to wear clothes. They liked to dress up for show; but did not see why they should be dressed all the time. Those who wore no clothing laughed at them, and told them they were spoiling their skins and would soon become spotted like leopards. Many of the natives are prouder of their black skin than of any clothes you can give them. Indeed, as long as they have a good supply of jewelry to wear, they do not mind their nakedness. They say, "Them close he no be we-fashion."

When our work opened in Garraway the prospects for a successful school seemed very good, since one thing necessary to success is that all parties concerned in an undertaking should be intensely interested in it. Our people in Garraway, both young and old, were much interested in the mission, and for the first six months we were more than busy with teaching, both during and after school hours. But when we went to Garraway the people were talking of war with a neighboring tribe. After we had been there a few months they began to keep guard night and day, and in November, 1889, they fought the first battle. Many of the children's relatives were killed and others wounded in the fight, and for two reasons our school had to be closed: first, the children were called home by their parents, who did not consider it safe to leave them with me, since the mission was so near the enemy; and, secondly, our people sent for me to come and care for their wounded, and I was obliged to spend much of my time in town. Both old and young were so excited over the war that scarcely a person could think of books. Night and day the enemy was expected.

After the first two battles two of our young men, who were anxious to learn and knew that the war would not be easily or quickly settled, came for a lesson whenever they were not on guard or had no other work to do. Many an hour I spent with these two pupils, carefully explaining to them every word, teaching them Bible stories and the truths of God, telling them of Jesus and the better way, and talking to them of the wonderful ways in which God had delivered his people that trusted in him in the past. These were the only two young men in our tribe who did not go to the devil-doctor to obtain charms and "medicine" to protect them from the bullets. Both are living to-day and belong to our church. One of them is the interpreter of our mission.

Always when I went to town I carried a book with me, and whenever I met our boys and young men I would give them a short lesson or review the old ones, that they might not forget what they had learned. Often I spent hours teaching these individual lessons both from our schoolbooks and from the Bible, instilling into the minds of the young that there was a better way for them than the one their fathers had followed for so many generations, and assuring them that if they would accept Jesus as their Master and God's law as their guide they would have no more war. God's law, I told them, was that we should love one another.

As I look back now to those days I will remember what a trial for me it used to be to go into the towns alone among a lot of rough, rude, heathen soldiers, many of them half drunk, and speaking a language that I could not understand. How their shrieks and yells used to make the cold chills run over me! Yet I knew I was safe, for God was with me and had sent me to teach them a better way. I felt that the only way to accomplish the work I had come to do was to heed our Saviour's command, "Go out into the highways and hedges, and compel them to come in," resting on the promise, " Lo, I am with you alway." I never shall cease to praise God for his manifest presence with me. Many times I realized the fulfillment of the promise, when everything human and temporal made me realize that I was in a strange land and among a strange people, yet I never felt alone.

After peace returned we took our children back to school and encouraged all the young men to study. But many of our most interesting pupils were no longer there. They had fallen in the war—our interpreter among the rest. Moreover, many of the young men were sad and never took up their books again. The adults were weak from the scanty food they had eaten during the troubled time. Few had the ambition to follow out a new idea, finding it was all that they could do to get their farm-work started again. However, the children we had adopted—or, I ought to say, the boys, for at this time we had no girls—were under our immediate control and we had them regularly in school. They did very well under the circumstances, and many a weary, yet happy and encouraging, day I have spent with my Garraway boys.

CHAPTER III.

THE WAR.

A War Cloud.—The Struggle for the Coast.—An Old Sore. —Two Causes of Contention, Territory and Women.— Closing the Thoroughfare.—The Sword Fight.—Amateur Surgery.— The Rout of the Nemia People.—Gunshot Wounds.—Bob Charcoal's Death.

WHEN we first came to Garraway we were impressed with the disturbed and restless condition of the people. When we landed on the beach that first night, we could see by the light of the moon that the men carried guns, and we at once thought of war. When we went up to the mission house a number of these warriors —every able-bodied Garraway man is a soldier —went along carrying their guns on their bare, black shoulders. The coast people are somewhat in advance of those in the interior, and for years they have fought with guns, instead of bows and arrows. Liberia extends only fifty miles back from the coast, and all the tribes have had sufficient contact with civilization to appreciate the superiority of firearms.

The first morning in our new home, all ages and sizes of the people came to see us. The men still had their firearms, and as we did not like so many guns in the house, they left them outside, leaning against the posts of the house. Indeed, our house, standing six feet from the ground, often looked more like a soldiers' drill shed than a Methodist mission house.

In response to our inquiries we learned that the Peddie people, a tribe which once lived on the coast, but which our people had driven into the bush, were making the disturbance by threatening to return to their old haunts. The Garraway people had offered them a site for a town, but they were not willing to accept it as a favor. Another neighboring tribe, the Nemia people, had induced the Peddies to unite in a war against the Garraway people, hoping thus to be able to drive them from the coast and come into possession of their territory.

Another reason why the Peddie people had declined the location offered them by the Garraway people was because it lay between the two largest Garraway towns, and they wanted a settlement entirely to themselves. This the Garraways were not willing to allow, knowing the Peddies to be a most treacherous people, and were willing to let them come to the coast only on condition that they live among the Garraways as friends, and not settle down by themselves. To allow them to do this would

THE WAR. 49

only give them an opportunity to make trouble.

The Peddie people had never forgiven the Garraways for conquering them, and the Nemia people had a grievance because some of their women had run away and were living with our tribe. Fearing lest they might not be able to succeed, the allies invited some of their neighbors to help them; and the Genoer, Nyambo, and Fishtown tribes, making five in all, joined in the war.

Our people often told me the story of their wars, and how they themselves were once driven from the beach by the Liberian people. After living eight years in the bush—I have often passed the place where their town used to be, on my way up into the interior—they paid a a heavy fine to the government and returned to the beach. They had a few years of peace, and then began the contention that has never ceased. It will be necessary to give its history to enable the reader to understand the events which followed.

In former years the Nemia, Garraway, and Peddie people lived in peace along the coast, the Garraway people being between the other two tribes. Early one morning an outside enemy attacked the Nemia town, and our people, according to promise, rushed out to help their neighbors. Our king, who was a far-seeing man, warned his subjects to be ready to defend themselves. But in their haste and excitement they forgot the warning.

But no sooner had they started than their neighbors and supposed friends, the Peddie people, stole into the defenseless village and set it on fire, hoping in this way to drive the Garraways back to their old homes in the bush. Fortunately, however, the smoke was early discovered, and our people rushed back in time to put out the fire and save their homes from destruction. They pursued the Peddies back to their own town. But the Peddies fled to the bush rather than risk a battle; and there they built new homes and continued to live, nursing their hatred against the tribe which had deprived them of their coastland, and ready for any enterprise which should restore them to their own.

There are two main causes of the almost unceasing warfare which is the history of the Liberian tribes. One is the desire for more territory; for the land is not definitely allotted, and between the tribes lie tracts, usually heavily timbered, which furnish building materials, lumber, thatch, and "tie-tie"—the rope which takes the place of nails. This common ground is a bone of perpetual contention. The other source of discord is "the woman question." The native men buy their women, and have as many wives as they can pay for; the more wives a man has the more respected he is. Many of these women take no interest in their families, and after a trifling dispute with their husbands will run away to other tribes to become the wives of other men. To lose a wife is to lose an investment; and the first husband accuses the new one of dishonesty, unless he returns her value in money. This a member of a hostile tribe will not do. So the quarrel gets hotter and hotter, until the two tribes are in open war. In the present case our people told us that they wanted no war, and should not be the first to begin hostilities, but if they were fired on they would protect their homes and lives.

Some time previously the Garraway and Nemia people, who were originally one tribe, met together and offered sacrifice to their gods. Then they buried a gun, and every warrior turned his gun downward; and they declared before their gods that they were brothers and would never fight each other again. This treaty was faithfully kept for a number of years. But when we arrived in the beginning of 1889 the Nemia people had threatened to attack the Garraways unless they granted the Peddies a place on the beach by themselves. Our people were in readiness, for they had suspected treachery. The road taken by the two allied tribes in visiting each other was through Garraway territory, and the Garraways now forbade their further use of it. After that no man's life was safe on this road; but for a while the women were allowed to go back and forth unmolested. Soon, however, even they were forbidden to pass.

Our young men, when they came to the mission for their lessons, were always on the watch for these women. The mission being situated on a hilltop, was a good lookout for them, and many a lesson was cut short as they sighted women passing along that road. In an instant they would drop book or slate, and without a word of explanation rush out of the house and away down the hillside as fast as they could go. Most of them seemed pleased whenever they found that the women were not of a hostile tribe; but some seemed not at all pleased, for they would have preferred to show their patriotism by sending the women back empty-handed. I have seen our men stop a company of these women who were carrying loads of vegetables and other articles of food on their heads, take away everything they had, and send them back with threats that if they ever passed that way again it would go worse with them. The Garraways would never eat the things they had taken, for fear of poison, but would dig a hole and bury them just as they were. After the road was closed to them the women used to pass during the night, but with great caution and fear, lest they should be caught and imprisoned or tortured.

Both our people and the enemy were constantly defying each other, and scarcely a week passed without several warlike messages being exchanged between them. It was no longer safe for the women to go to the bush alone after wood, or to the vegetable farm for food. The people on the beach do not cultivate rice farms in time of war, since to do so they would be compelled to go to a distance and leave their homes unprotected. Consequently, war always brings famine. Our people suffered much from this cause, not having enough to eat. Day and night they kept on guard. The women did all the planting that was done, but while so engaged were kept in constant terror, not knowing at what time they might meet the ambushed enemy.

For several weeks before a battle was fought the guards used to walk until morning through the long grass and the bushes between the mission and their towns, blowing their war horns and ringing their war bells, that the enemy might know they were not asleep. They erected barricades at places where they feared the enemy might attempt to pass. These bullet-proof barricades were made of the stalks of banana trees, which are from eight to twelve inches thick, and were built like a hollow wall and were filled with sand, leaving small loopholes through which to fire at the enemy.

A war fence was built round each of our towns —not a very strong fence, for they had no heavy timber at hand and could not venture out to the big bush for heavy sticks. I have since seen very strong war fences in the interior where timber was plenty. The timber was cut from five to eight inches thick and about fourteen feet long, a trench was dug, and the timbers set endwise into the ground close together and bound with strong rope. I have seen war fences of this sort, whose gates were always shut at night, that it would have been hard work to break down without artillery. I often heard the enemy come out of their towns to where our people could hear them, and then, with their war horns, curse and taunt them and call them every insulting name they could think of.

One morning about ten o'clock they called

our people out to fight, and our people, to show they were not cowards, went out, with gun and sword, to meet them. After many hard words they began to cut at one another with their swords; and after two hours of blows of this kind they both returned to their towns.

Our people sent a man to summon me to dress their wounds. I took bandages, sticking plaster, some arnica, a needle and thread, and a pair of scissors. Asking God to give me all the grace and strength I should need for the duty, I went to town, and found first one of our head warriors with his head wrapped in a cloth red with blood. It was, indeed, a trial to me, as I had always shrunk from anything of the sort; but the people stood all around, no one seeming to know what to do. I leaned hard on Jesus, and he sustained me. I took off the cloth and found three great sword gashes on the top of the wounded man's head. The next thing was to get a razor and shave the hair off his head. They brought me an old, dull one. I went to work and shaved or scraped off the hair the best I could, until I could get the sticking plaster to hold the cuts together. Then I applied some medicine, bandaged the head, persuaded the man to lie down and be quiet, and went on to the next patient.

A young man had sat down beside me when

I began on the first case. But he was bleeding badly, and soon got too weak to sit up any longer, so they took him to his father's house, where I found him. I took off the bandages and found a great gash in his cheek, and another over the shoulder blade. He had been passing a tree, when, looking back, he saw close behind him one of the enemy with his sword upraised; and before he could get away the man, with one stroke of his sword, had cut a great gash down through his cheek and shoulder. The point of the sword had made a cut in his face three inches long and almost through to the teeth. After cleansing this thoroughly, since there is always danger that the blades may have been poisoned, I drew the wound carefully together with needle and thread, applied remedies, and bandaged it up. Then I dressed the gash on his shoulder, and went on to the next sufferer.

For weeks I did not for a day miss being in the town, and I spent more time caring for the wounded than in school. Those that could came to the mission when I could not stay in town long enough to attend to them all. I had no one to leave with the children, and could not always take them with me.

On the fifth of November, about two weeks after this first battle, I was awakened very early by loud talking. Our people had started out to surprise the Nemia town, but, finding they were not going to reach the place before daylight, had come back and were arguing together down at the foot of our hill. Finally they went home. But about noon the Nemia and Peddie warriors came out together and challenged our people to a battle with swords. Our people went out to meet them, still saying that they would not be the first to fire a gun, though every man carried one.

I heard the first sound of the war horn; and, going to the door where I could observe plainly all that was passing, I saw the Nemia people not far from our town. The Garraways gathered from all their towns. I saw them marching out to meet the enemy. I could see their swords glittering in the sun, and hear their shouts and the sound of the war horn and bells.

The enemy, scattered in a long line, with gun in hand, waited till our people came close enough to take good aim at our principal men. Then they fired. The first volley killed one of our best men, and his son, who was just behind him. This was a great blow to our people, and yet God used it for good. No other man that had gone into the battle carried so many charms and so much "medicine." He had been to a number of devil-doctors and they had all told him that the " medicine " they had given him was sufficient to protect him in battle, and that no ball could penetrate his skin while he wore the charms they had given him. When our people saw this man and others fall they were frightened, for all but two of them had gone trusting for their lives to the " medicine " they wore.

But, while they had reason to fear, the enemy had yet more reason. They remembered the treaty promise they had made, never to kill their brothers. God was their witness and the judge between them, and by being the first to break the law they felt that they had lost his favor. Their courage failed them; and, although they had had the advantage in firing the first shot and killing one of our best men, yet the consciousness of having broken their oath made their hearts sink. The Garraway people, on the other hand, felt that, according to the covenant between them, victory was theirs, and they took fresh courage. Sheathing their swords, they took their guns and began to fire.

From the door of the mission house I saw the first gun fired and heard the shots which followed in quick succession. I knew when our people began to fire, and could see them slowly driving the enemy back. After two hours of fighting with guns, swords, daggers, and cannon I saw the smoke begin to rise from the enemy's town. Then I knew that our tribe had been victorious and driven the enemy back to the town, then out of it, and had set it on fire.

Before any fighting had taken place the young men had talked of the day when they would be on the battlefield, and I had said, "If you fight I am going to come to town." They had told me not to come until I saw that they had fired the enemy's town and the smoke came up black. Then I might know that the town was well destroyed and the enemy had fled. So, when I saw the town on fire I got ready medicines and bandages, and when the smoke became black I went to town. It was about two o'clock in the afternoon when I got there. I found many of the wounded soldiers, and at once set to work to dress their wounds.

Some were shot in the leg, some in the trunk, and some in the arm. Some of the wounds had the bullets still in them, and we took them out with a penknife. The mission carpenter, who was working on a house near the town, was there before me and had already bound up several of the wounds. We both worked all afternoon, being called first to one place and then another. One man was shot between the eyes and seemed a hopeless case, although he lived for several days in great suffering.

Our first interpreter had promised to trust God, and not the " medicine." But his mother, fearing for him, had gone to the devil-doctor and inquired about her son's safety. The doctor had told her not to let him go to the war. But he, not willing to believe the devil-doctor, declared he would go, nevertheless, and fight for his home and country. He accordingly went along with the rest, and, being in the front of the battle, was shot in the temple and brought back to town. He knew that his mother would be alarmed to see him carried, and so had two men take hold of his arms and help him walk. When the poor woman saw him she was wild with grief. I dressed his wound, but perceived at once that it was serious, and, in fact, I did not see how he could live. I took out several pieces of bone; and we washed the wound well, to guard against possible poison.

Eight men who had gone out to battle had died on the field, and twenty-two had fallen in the towns on the beach, while a number more in the bush towns were wounded. So the towns were filled with the groans of the wounded and mourning for the dead. I never witnessed such a sight or heard such wailing as I did that day; and I hope, so long as I may be spared to labor in Africa, I may never meet the same again.

It was long after dark when I started for home. The mission carpenter had already gone, and I could get no person to go with me to the mission, for the towns were all in confusion, every man either wounded or on guard or burying the dead or busy about something. There was no hope of getting anyone to accompany me that night. I started alone. It was so dark that I could scarcely see to keep the narrow footpath among the bushes and grass. It is in such hours that I have tested the power and presence of God to keep me. And how wonderfully he has done it and brought me through all these most trying periods! To his name be all the praise! When I reached home the children had had their supper, and I sat down and ate something; but, hungry as I was, I was so tired I could scarcely eat.

Just as we were ready for bed, our presiding elder and his wife came in from up the coast. They had been thirty-six hours in the boat without food or water, and were quite overcome from exposure to the tropical sun and the cool night air. We got something for them to eat, and then all retired to rest. They went on their way to the Cape in the morning, and I went to the town to attend to the sick.

Many of our mission children had friends killed in the war, and their people called them home to mourn with them; therefore, I had only two little boys to teach. As I found that I could not spend much time at home—being continually summoned to town—I let these two little boys go to their own people for a time, leaving with me one boy of another tribe and an old man. It was impossible to attend to the wounded and do anything in the mission house.

When I went to town I found that our interpreter, "Bob Charcoal"—a name which the traders had given him because he was so very black—had become very weak. I took him a cup of tea, which he drank; and I dressed his wound, talked with him a few minutes, and then went on to attend to the rest. I had gone to another town to attend to patients there, when a woman came running up and shouted at the top of her voice that Bob was dead. I went back at once to where he was, and found the people standing around the house. I forced my way through the crowd and into the house.

It was a little hut about twelve feet square,

and full of women, with a fire in the center, and three old women holding Bob up in the corner. It was so hot and smoky that I could remain but a few minutes. I forced my way to Bob, looked into his face, and saw that he was not dead, but was almost smothered. I rushed out and told some of the men that he was alive, and that they must bring him outside. They went in, shoving the screaming women aside. The uproar was deafening. The women, far from imagining that they themselves were smothering him to death, believed that by hiding him away in the little hut he would be safe from the witches, and that keeping him beside that smoky fire was his only chance for life. Their crowding round him and their cries were to show him that he was much appreciated, and that they were all very sorry to lose him.

I ran for water, since I knew that in such excitement there was no hope of getting anybody to send for it. I found some in a house near by. When I came back, the men had Bob outside. I made all the women stand back and stop their screaming, while I bathed him with cold water until he revived. Then I told the people to take him to his own house, and that I would take care of him myself. So they carried him home, and we put him to bed.

I told the king, who was his uncle, that the townspeople must not be allowed to come around and make a noise. We kept them reasonably quiet so long as I was there, but the great trouble in time of sickness with these people is to get any person to assume responsibility. The nearest friend, even the mother, if she should show any uncommon attention to her son, might be accused of witching him and taken out and subjected to the deadly ordeal of the "sasswood." It is impossible to have a sick person cared for, unless you do it yourself. The people are likely to have him sitting up close by the fire, or lying on the bare ground outside, or to bathe him thoroughly in hot water. I could not bear the thought of Bob's dying from neglect; so I took my cot bed to town, put it up in his house, and stayed by him all night. He was very restless, and all the next day suffered much. I left him only to attend to my other patients.

The fifth day he was unconscious part of the time, but at other times I talked with him a little when he was quiet. He had told me before that if the people buried him, it would be all right, for he was "God's man," and was going to live in heaven with God. I read and prayed with him every day, and we used to talk of God and heaven. The last night, after we had had prayer, he said, "Now, I want you to say that chapter all over, and let me say it after you." So I repeated it, a few words at a time, and he repeated it after me. It was the seventy-first Psalm—one that had been given to him for a lesson when he used to come to school. After repeating it all over, he prayed in his native language. The king was sitting near him, and called to him until he answered him. I said, "King, Bob was praying, wasn't he?" The king did not answer me; but Bob replied, "I was. Ask him what he stopped me for."

He fell asleep for a while, but was restless all night. Some of the soldiers were returning from the watch during the night, and called in to see how he was. He had been suffering much, and wanted to turn over while they were there. I asked them to help him; but not one of them would touch him, for they believe if a soldier going to war should touch a wounded man he would be sure to be wounded himself when he went into battle. So Bob, seeing that none would help him, made a desperate attempt and stood straight up in his bed. His sister and I got him to lie down, but he was quite exhausted and never spoke after that. At eleven o'clock the next morning he died without a struggle, resting quietly as if asleep.

Men, women, and children cried when they heard that Bob was dead, for he was loved and respected by all. I felt as sad as if my own brother had died, for he had been a brother to me; and I sat down and cried with the rest. The people were kind to me and felt sorry for me. One of the chiefs took me by the hand and led me away from the house, to his own, where they put up my bed and told me I should lie down and rest, but must not cry.

They began at once to prepare to bury him; for it is their custom in war time not to keep their dead, but bury them at once. They took a canoe and made a coffin out of it, and soon were ready to lay the body away. They came to call me, and said that I must bring "the Book" and read. I did not know how I could speak or read through my tears; but they urged me to go. I asked God to give me grace for that special duty, and, through sobs and tears, I read a part of the seventy-first Psalm—the one Bob had repeated the night before he died. I held in my hand the Bible I had given to Bob; it was all soiled at the places where he had studied his lessons.

He was buried within two hours after he died, as there was danger of the enemy attacking them, and there was no time for their heathen rites. They buried him among the chiefs, on the beach, although he was not more than twenty-seven years old, and, according to their custom, was called "a small boy." But he was a man of such principle, and was so liked by all, that they buried him by the side of a king who had died in battle.

The afternoon was wet, and I could not go home. I was so tired and worn-out from sitting up at night that I felt I must have a rest or I should be sick myself. So the next day I returned to the mission and went to bed. In the morning I went to see the sick again. For two or three days I spent most of my time in the town, coming home at night. I had lost so much sleep that I was weary; but the thoughts of the war and the sufferings of the people often kept me long awake.

CHAPTER IV.

THE END OF THE WAR.

The Famine.—Dethroning a King.—A Night Alarm.—Bestman's Bravery.—Woe to the Vanquished.—The Devil-doctor's Money.—End of the War.—"The Spewing of the Water."

ONE day when I was in town a letter came to the king, who called me to read it. It was from a friendly tribe at Cape Palmas, warning him that the Fishtown people were going to bring war against him by sea.

Our people began to look so worn, weary, and thin that it was very evident they were famishing. I felt that many of the hungry ones were not likely to see Christmas, now not many days distant, and, if they did, would not be able to enjoy the day, on account of the war. I thought the greatest kindness I could do to them would be to give them something to eat. I baked a few loaves of bread, measured out half a sack of rice, some tea, dried apples, and sugar, also a bag of potatoes, and sent word to the king that he must send up to the mission to get them, so that they might have a dinner. He sent up six men to get the things and to thank me. Many thanks I received the next day when I went to town.

All was war palaver in town. They had accused the king of witching the war, and two of the devil-doctors of making medicine to kill their own people. Everybody was excited. Men and woman came down from the bush towns of our tribe to talk this war palaver. The women did the principal part of the talking. The people all sat down in the sun before the king's house at ten o'clock; and, although there came a heavy shower of rain, they did not move their seats, but talked on through it all. Some of the women are great talkers and can hold the attention of all the people. Although the king denied the charge, yet many of the people believed him guilty and threatened his life if any more lives were lost in the war.

That night the king, fearing the anger of the people, started to run away, but was caught by the people as he was crossing the river to the other tribe. They tied him hand and foot, put him in the top of a small hut, built a fire, and threw red pepper into it. They smothered the flames to smoke with green grass and bushes, and, shutting the door, left the poor creature there until morning, when he fell down to the floor through the hole in the ceiling through which they had put him up.

They untied him then; but he was so stiff and stupid that he could scarcely move. When he felt better they again asked him whether he was guilty or not. Knowing that the people would take no explanation, he said that he was, but would make some "medicine" to counteract all the witchcraft he had used in the war. They kept him shut up all day, but let him go to his own house that night.

The next day, being Sunday, I went to one of the small towns to hold service. We had not been able to have service for several weeks, since the excited people could not be induced to sit together in one place; and it was seldom they were in town, for all the smaller towns had to be guarded. I had just got a congregation together and started the service when there came a man who called all the people to the king's town for palaver. My meetings were at an end for that day, and I went with the rest to hear the palaver. It was about the king's witching the war, and the warriors were furious. Some of them wished to take the ring off his ankle and take him out and kill him. But he begged them so hard not to do it that they left him to make the "medicine" which he had said would counteract all the witchcraft and give them sure success.

I had been in the habit of taking one day for rest and letting the children go to the river to fish. But since the war had begun I had had no rest day, for many people called at the mission, and I never liked to refuse to see them. In those war times I felt that possibly I should never see them again or have another chance to urge them to accept Jesus Christ as their Saviour.

One morning the king passed our house without coming in. I asked him to stop, but he said he was going to find some "medicine" and would be back soon. So I set the tea on the stove, as I knew he would be sure to want a drink of tea and something to eat on his way home; for he was always hungry. I looked for him for some time, but he did not come. I thought that he had perhaps gone home by another way and was making the "medicine" for the war.

Just as it was growing dark he came, and stood for a few minutes under the house, listening to discover whether any of his persecutors were there. One of my boys came to tell me that the king had arrived. I at once felt that something was the matter, for these people do not like to be out in the dark if they can help it.

I went out and met him just as he came into the house. It was almost dark. I asked, "Is this you, king?" "Yes," he answered; "is there anyone in the house?" I told him there was no person but our family, and invited him to sit down. He said the people had been all ready to kill him in the morning; but he had run away and had been in the bush all day without anything to eat. He had two *cassadas* in his hand, and asked me to cook them for him. We made a fire and got something for him to eat. He asked to stay all night. I told him he could, but inquired what he meant to do in the morning. He said that he intended to run away and never come back to the country again.

When a man is made king a metal ring is put on his ankle as a sign of his authority; and this ring belongs to the tribe and is handed down from one generation to another. I asked him whether it would not be a good thing for him to take the ring off his foot and leave it with me. I would take it, I said, to the people in the morning and tell them that I had seen him, and that he had gone to another tribe; and I would beg them not to search for him. "Yes," he said. If it had not been for the ring on his foot he would have gone far away that day, but by the anklet any person he met would know that he was a king, and he would be more easily found out. I got down on the floor and, with a pair of pincers, unwound the wire that fastened the ring.

After supper I gave him matches and a blanket to wrap himself in and prepared him for his journey. He had a dagger with him. He said he was going to sleep in the bush and would take some vegetables from the farm as he passed along. He wanted the matches to light a fire to roast them. He lay down on his mat to sleep, but asked me to let the lamp burn by him. He kept his dagger by his side, and was so nervous that he would start at the least sound. None of us slept much that night. At four o'clock I got up and got something for him to eat, and he started off before daylight. He intended never to return to his home again, but hoped to meet some friendly tribe with whom he might live out the rest of his days, which would not be many, for he was already an old man.

About eight o'clock his brother came up to the mission to see whether I knew anything about the king. I showed him the king's ring, related what I knew, and told him that I was only waiting for the dew to dry off the grass before coming down to bring the ring and explain that the king was gone.

When I went to town they called the warriors together. I gave them the anklet and, telling them what had passed at our house, asked them not to follow the king, but let him go in peace. They thanked me many times for taking the ring off the king's foot and bringing it to them, saying I had done them a good service.

The king wandered on for three days, crawling through the thick bushes at night and hiding away during the day, that he might not be found by his own tribe. But when he was near the place where he was going for refuge, a hunter discovered him, and he was brought to one of the bush towns of our own people. They were kind to him, keeping him for several months, and finally making peace between him and his own town people and bringing him again to his former home. For many months he had no power at all among the people. At length, however, the devil-doctor declared that the devil was not pleased with the way they had treated their king, and wished them to put the ring on his foot again. Accordingly a sacrifice was offered to the devil for the wrong they had done, and the ring was restored to the king's foot; and he wore it until he died two years later.

On a Saturday I was awakened just as it began to grow light, by the firing of guns. I threw open the window—not a glazed sash, but a rough board shutter—and looked out to see what was the matter at that early hour. I found that the enemy had come by stealth and seemed to be in one of our small towns. There was a force of about eighty men; and in quick succession they fired their guns. I heard the screams and cries of our people. I feared they would burn the town that morning, and kill many of the people, for I knew that this town was not so well fortified as the others, and I remembered that on account of its location it was not guarded as closely as the others. The foe had come in by a back road, and had reached the fence, which was only fifteen feet from the first house in the town. Inside of this light fence was a barricade. For several days everything had been quiet, and no guard had been stationed there until that night.

In place of our dead interpreter we had chosen "Bestman," a young man who was anxious to learn and was one of the two who went through the war without "medicine," charms, or protection from the heathen gods. His mother's house was the nearest to the fence, and she had prevailed on her husband, the chief man in the town, to have a guard set at the barricade behind the house.

Bestman, so named because of his good qualities, was one of the four sentinels posted there. They thought it would be sufficient to watch only during the early hours of the morning, the most likely time for an attack. But Bestman could not sleep all night. Several times he was up. He had called the rest of the guard more than once. One of them was angry at being awakened "just when the gods were telling him something," as he said. He had placed his idols at his head when he lay down, that they might talk to him while he slept; and he believed the dreams that came to him were what the idols told him.

Only two of the watchers, Bestman and his brother, were in their places when the enemy appeared. A grove of palm trees had hidden them until they were near the town, and now that they were seen they were close to the fence. The two men at the barricade fired their guns and gave the alarm. The other two came at once, and met the leader of the enemy just entering the gate of the town. They fired, and he dropped dead. Another of the enemy began to hack at the fence with his sword, but was shot by a man who had rushed

THE END OF THE WAR. 77

to the help of the guard. Six others of our people fired; and the enemy, seeing that they were discovered and their leader was fallen, began to retrace their steps. I supposed from the dense powder smoke that the town must be burning. The noise was terrible: and in the still of the morning we could hear every sound.

In a few minutes I saw a crowd running from the town, and thought them our women and children fleeing for their lives. They came in the direction of the mission, and I soon discovered them to be the enemy, for they had guns in their hands. They went around the fence of our farm, over the hill into the swamp, and on to their own village.

The enemy had planned to take the small town that day, and to this end had divided their forces into three bodies, one advancing directly to the town in question, a second proceeding by another road to make a pretended attack upon the large town, and a third approaching in canoes as if to attack the king's town by sea. When the firing began in the small town the enemy showed themselves at the other two places. Every one of our men had to stand at his own post, and none could be spared to go to the help of the weaker village. The men who attacked the small town outnumbered the villagers three times, and could easily have taken the place, had it not been that God was set for the defense of our people. In this small town lived the two men who had trusted God through all the war; and I believe that God gave our people the victory to show them that it came not by might, but through his aid.

As soon as the enemy had passed I went at once to the town, feeling that surely there would be many killed and wounded after so much firing at close range. On the way I met several of our soldiers, who said to me, "O, teacher, nobody die, no man hurt." I went on with them to the town, and found the villagers gathering together to discuss the attack. The defenders of the town were running to and fro, and the women were taking up dust and throwing it over them, and were shouting and singing their praises.

I found our interpreter, Bestman, with his coat and trousers on. This was a remarkable thing for a native. Generally they cannot be induced to put on such clothes. All they wear is a small piece of cloth about the loins. When they go to battle they add their war charms, anything that will disguise them and make them look hideous, and cover their bodies with "war medicine," to make their skin bullet-proof; or it may be that this charm is to keep the balls from striking them at all.

The people crowded around Bestman, seeing him with his clothes on and knowing that he had been one of the brave guard. They would ask him if "for true" he had worn those clothes when the enemy came. When he answered that he had they would exclaim, "For true, true, God got strong. God help we to-day. If it no been God help we, our town done burn this time."

The leader of the enemy lay where he fell, just outside the fence. I went to look at him; and O, what a sight! Every soldier that passed had cut a gash in the body with his sword, until it was completely mangled, the arms and feet cut off, and the head laid open. Every additional passer-by displayed his bravery by bestowing one wound more.

Meanwhile the enemy were being pursued; and one of their men was found with both of his legs broken. He was most unmercifully hacked to pieces by our cruel-hearted warriors. They followed on and found another, who suffered as the first. Several guns were picked up on the road. A few days afterward they discovered another man, a deserter of their own people, who had been wounded in the assault and left in the swamp to die.

Three days after the battle our people found a young man with both his legs broken. He had crawled at night among the bushes until he was nearly home. The young warriors who found him cut his head off and brought it to town in great triumph. But the old men were not pleased with them, and said that he should have been brought in alive and made to tell the plans of the enemy and how their towns were fortified.

One evening a woman came from Nemia to be the wife of one of our men. Our people were rejoiced to receive one who could give them information of their enemies. They fired eight guns that night and four in the morning, as a sign to the enemy that they had received the woman and were exulting over it.

There were ten devil-doctors in our tribe, who made much "medicine" in time of war. But the people feared defeat if they trusted to their medicine alone, and had sent for a more famous devil-doctor who lived several miles away. He had been with our tribe for months, and had been given everything he asked for, as an inducement to make "medicine" that would surely give them victory.

They had given him bullocks in return for the charms and idols he had made. Some of these he had sold and intended taking the money home with him. But one night when he was drunk he lost it. When he became sober he missed it and accused some of our people of stealing it. He was very angry, and said that nothing should be done in the town until his money was found. He even forbade the women going for water or cooking. Everything in the village came to a standstill. The town was searched, and the accused persons were threatened with having to drink "sasswood" if the money was not found before a certain day.

After a general uproar, much excitement, and many hard words one of his own wives—for he had brought three of his ten wives with him—confessed to having taken the money while he lay in a drunken stupor. She had feared lest he should spend it all, and she get none. The people were much offended by the way he had acted, but were glad to have the truth known at last.

In spite of their victories the people remained in constant fear. The enemy far outnumbered them, and they stood in constant danger of attack. For some time all the soldiers slept in the bush outside the town, and some of the women slept across the river with a friendly tribe—the Po River people.

The devil-doctor counseled the Garraways

to wait until he should consult the devil as to the best time for attacking the remaining towns. But one day the Po River people came over and told our people that they were tired of the war and were going to make an end of it. The devil-doctor objected to their fighting on that day and urged them to wait for him; but the people answered that they meant to let nothing stop them. They were determined to burn the other towns and make an end of the war that day.

Accordingly they put "medicine" in their guns and on their skins, and set out. Their departure was not known to all the people; for some of the young men who happened to be at the mission house knew nothing about it until they saw the smoke. Then we listened and heard the firing. The young men ran to town for their guns and then started to join their comrades; and I soon followed to see what I could find to do. One man had been killed, and five were wounded. They had fallen upon the enemy unexpectedly and entered their town with little difficulty, but few sentinels being on guard. The other allied tribes had gone home to get ready for a fresh attack, and the men of the town were compelled to retreat, leaving the women and children to flee to the bush for safety. Our people that day burned three towns they had left at the time of the previous battle, and then returned to their own homes jubilant over their victories.

The enemy was thoroughly defeated, their homes being burned. The Peddies had begun the war; and they and their friends, the Nemia people, had been defeated and lost their homes, and they realized that there was no use in fighting any longer. Our people, being in control of the beach, had forbidden any trade with their enemies in the interior, thus depriving the bush people of many commodities, and especially salt, which they prize very highly.

Our people kept a close guard over the captured places, and soon began to build a new town for themselves on the site of one of the Nemia towns they had burned. This was according to the covenant made between the tribes when they had called the gods to witness that they would never fight again. That the enemy might be discouraged from all hope of returning, our people cut down all the cocoanut, plum, and other fruit trees planted by the Nemia people.

One morning, about two weeks later, to the great delight of our people, the Peddie tribe sent two women to acknowledge for them that they were defeated and ask for peace. They came first to our bush towns and then down to the beach. One of the women held a small native-made ax in her hand, and went around to all our towns holding it over her head and calling out, " Dwa oh ! dwa oh ! dwa oh ! "— which is their way of confessing themselves conquered and of begging for pardon.

That was a day of rejoicing. Our people sent the women back with a message to their tribe that, if they really wished for peace, two of their soldiers should come down and make " medicine," and then our people would send men to make medicine in the Peddie town.

One rite that has to be performed as a part of any reconciliation is what is called "the spewing of water." All parties concerned meet together, fill a basin with cold water, and each in turn lifts some of the water in his hands to his mouth. Then he blows it out upon the palms of the hands of the other party. This is done by each party three times, these words being repeated : " I do this to show that I wash myself from all the past. We shall be friends from this day."

It is the native law that those defeated in war shall pay a fine to the conquering tribe. This the Peddies and Nemias have not done, and consequently to-day the tribes live as enemies, although they have not been in open warfare since 1889.

CHAPTER V.

LIBERIA—ITS PEOPLE, LANGUAGES, AND CUSTOMS.

The Government of Liberia.—Means of Livelihood.—The Native Peoples.—Native Kings.—Pode Seere.—"Witching."—An African "Coronation"—Kalenky.—The Po River King.—A Revolution.—A Royal Exile.

THE republic of Liberia lies in western Africa, on what is known as the Grain Coast. It is about three hundred miles in length along the Atlantic and extends fifty miles back into the interior. It was founded as a home for emancipated slaves from the United States of America, and its laws are modeled upon those of that republic. The Liberian flag is somewhat like the American, though it has but a single star. The American Colonization Society organized and sustained the settlements until 1847, when an independent form of government was adopted, which was recognized by most of the nations of the earth. There are an elective president, vice president, and legislature, and a well-organized system of judiciary and of trial by jury; and besides there are governors for the counties and mayors for the towns.

These Liberian citizens are quite separate from the natives. Many of them have learned the languages of the natives, but their own language is the English. Some of the men are excellent mechanics. The farmers raise chiefly vegetables, as well as some coffee and sugar cane, from which last they make molasses, and occasionally a little brown sugar.

The principal means of support is by trading with the natives for the products of their country. A number of the Liberians do a good business as merchants. They go up and down the coast and rivers in surfboats, taking to the natives rice, tobacco, fish, powder, firearms, rum, salt, brass kettles, iron pails, beads, basins, crockery, and other manufactured articles, which they exchange for palm oil, palm kernels, fowls, ivory, rubber, camwood, walnut, and other kinds of wood.

The law of Liberia allowing the white man neither to own land nor to become a citizen of the republic gives the whites no interest in the country beyond an opportunity of making all they can out of its people by trading. White residents are in Liberia only for the sake of money, and care nothing for the welfare of the people or the good of the country.

Christian missionaries have done much in the way of teaching the people. To the different societies of the church of God Liberia owes its present condition. The people have received almost all their education at the hands of the different missionary societies.

The native peoples of Liberia are very easily distinguished from those Liberians who are descended from the emancipated American slaves. They live in native huts, built according to the pattern of their fathers. They are subject to the government of the republic in some things, yet have their own customs and settle their own private disputes. Rarely except in case of war do they apply to the government for protection, and rarely are they consulted by the president, except in matters of common interest.

In every native tribe there is the first, or head, king, for all the people. His office corresponds to that of the president of the republic. In every town there is, besides, a local king, corresponding to the mayor in a civilized town. There are also chiefs in all the towns, who are the king's assistants; and all matters of dispute or difficulties of any kind among the people come before the king and chiefs of the town. Whatever cannot be settled by this council is taken before the head king, and all the other kings and chiefs make up the royal council.

The kingship belongs to a certain family.

But when we speak of a family in Liberia we mean the whole family connection, or clan, for the natives live much as the children of Israel used to live, many households having some one man whom they all look up to and call their father, the whole family bearing his name. Any member of this family may be chosen king by the people, and if he fails to give satisfaction his office may be taken from him and another appointed in his place. But the new king must be of the same family; none other can hold the office.

Some years ago our king died, and for a time the Garraway people on the beach got along without a king. During this period they discussed the question who was the proper person to rule over them. Two men were suggested. One was a young man named Pode Seere. But some objected to him on account of his youth, and others because he was given to drink. When Pode Seere was a boy his father had been king and had been greatly loved by all the people; but when the small-pox had swept through the land he had been numbered among its victims.

The people had a law that no person should cry when any of the people died of this pest, for great numbers were perishing, and it was said that the mourning only made the plague worse. They had restrained their feelings, and seen many of their dear ones fall by the terrible disease; but when their king died they all burst out in a wail for him. They would cry now, they said, for they were all dead.

The ravages of smallpox had left them few and weak, and a devil-doctor had prophesied that the tribe would never prosper until their late king's son should become king. Pode Seere, his only son, was at this time quite a lad. Another member of the royal family was made king; but he, too, died, and his successor was deposed because a jealous rival persuaded the people that he was always "making witch" and using his influence with the devils to defeat anything they wished to accomplish. This cunning rival was then made king, that he might exert his influence with the devils for good. This man was king when I went to Garraway, and he died three years ago.

After thoroughly discussing who should be chosen the next king, all the chiefs met in council to decide what should be done. A number of them were chosen to consult the devil-doctor. They took with them the man whom they had selected as the most capable man among them to rule. The devil-doctor said that this was the man whom the devil approved, no doubt having heard whom the people wanted. After making several new idols and a number of charms, the devil-doctor sent the chiefs home, the monarch-elect of course not having heard all the discussion.

The chiefs reached home the same day, and kept their own counsel. But in the night, when all were asleep, a number of the principal ones went quietly to the town where the man whom they had selected—Kalenky—lived, awakened him and his wife, and told them that he was to be their king and must come with them to the royal house, which was in another town. So they quietly took Kalenky and his head wife—Doladdy—and lodged them, as king and queen, in the king's house, built in the town where the king always lives. No one but the chiefs knew what was done until the next morning. When the people of Kalenky's village got up they missed their fellow-townsman. When they learned what had been done in the night they all sat down and cried for him, as if he had been dead, for he was a good man and they all liked him as a neighbor.

Certain ceremonies need to be performed and certain sacrifices offered when a new king is established. A steel ring is put upon his ankle as a mark of his authority. This anklet is a band of metal which has been beaten thin at several points and the edges brought together so as form little cups or bells. In each of these cups is a bit of loose metal, which tinkles when the wearer walks.

After the proper ceremonies had been completed and Kalenky acknowledged as king he began to move his boxes and other property to his new home. The queen was very sorry to leave her old home, and did not think that the honor made up for all the inconvenience and loneliness she had to endure. For weeks she might be found sitting on the floor and crying and lamenting over the calamity that had befallen her, of which some would have been very proud. After the rice was cut and the harvesting done, the king's son and nephew, who had lived beside him in his old home, moved from their own village and built near him. He also brought his other wives, and after some time he was again settled, and his head wife began to feel at home.

Soon afterward a new king's house was built for him, where he lived until the devil-doctor again declared a change to be necessary. Accordingly the people rose up one day, caught Pode Seere, took the ring off Kalenky's ankle, put it on Pode Seere, and declared him their king, believing that the fulfillment of the old devil-doctor's prophecy would bring them peace and prosperity. A king has very little authority among his people. They are very superstitious, and he can do little to improve the country or introduce better modes of living.

The king of our neighboring tribe, the Po River people, was an enterprising man, who had been down the coast and seen more of civilization than most of his subjects. He had a large family of sons, who were often away from home with the traders, and would bring back to their father cloth, powder, firearms, rum, and numbers of plates and bowls, with which the natives are fond of decorating their houses. They drill holes in these dishes, put a string through them, and hang them up in rows back of the waterpot. Most of the chiefs and principal men have their houses ornamented in this way. One family in our tribe thought to surpass all the rest. In order to do this every man in the family made palm oil and sold it to buy white soup plates and wash basins, all of which were put into one house. I counted them once and found five hundred and fifty, hanging in five rows round the wall. This is the largest house in the tribe; there would not have been room for so many on the wall of an ordinary house.

This king of Po River—Yaba was his name—instead of wasting the money his sons brought home, put it carefully away. The plates and basins he hung up for decoration in his own house, and his quarter of the town began to assume a greatly improved appearance. Everything was going on quietly, and he was encouraged to think that, perhaps, better days were in store for him and that he would be able to make further improvements which would be an example and inspiration to his people.

But his people began to look at him with suspicion. "What is Yaba trying to do?" said they. "This is not our country fashion. We never saw any man do this before in our country." The truth was they wanted to have a share in the earnings that the king's sons brought home, and were jealous of his fortune.

This year there had been a great deal of rain, and the rice crop was poor. So they declared that Yaba had witched the rice. For two days they quarreled; and on the third day I, with all the young men, went over to see if we could do anything for the king. We found the people in a great rage, the warriors gathered together in council, and the king sitting in the door of his house looking very sad. His sons were sitting around, unable to do anything to help their father.

They gave us seats, and we asked why there

should be so much disturbance among them. The king replied that the people had accused him of witching the rice and making it rot, and were determined to give him "sasswood," or else drive him away from his home. They had taken the ring off his foot and had stripped him of everything he had in his houses. The bowls and plates had all been taken down, and they had even compelled his family to give up many things of their own in order to atone for the harm done to the rice by his witchcraft.

The people had already eaten a bullock and a goat and were now cooking a dinner of chicken soup, rice, and vegetables. The warriors had been through the town and caught every fowl they could find that belonged to the king or to any of his relatives. As we went into the town I had seen a man come out of a house with one of these fowls which he had captured. Holding it up as high as he could, he swung it around by the neck in great triumph until the fowl's head was wrung off and its body dropped to the ground. He then picked it up and carried it to where a number of the young warriors were cleaning and preparing the fowls for cooking.

The king's head wife had carefully cultivated a little garden of *cassada* near her house, for use on a rainy day or in case strangers should come in unexpectedly. In a few minutes she could dig some of these roots and prepare a meal without going to the large farm a mile or two away. Her little garden was in better condition than that of any of the other women, and the *cassadas* were large and just ready for using. These cruel people had taken her *cassadas* for their dinner, and there the roots lay in a pile on the floor.

I stopped to talk to them about their doings and tried to persuade them to let their king remain alive in peace, for they all knew that he was a good man and had not harmed the rice. They did not want to listen, and kept up a perfect babble all the time I was talking. Some of them said they would put pepper in the fire and smoke me out, and one went out and brought back a basin half full of pepper. He set it down, however, because he knew I could better afford to leave the house than they, for they had brought their fowls and vegetables there to clean and cook.

After a time we went back to the king's house to see what could be done. Soon a crowd of furious warriors came to the house. Their leader held in his hand a whip of elephant hide. It was about three quarters of an inch thick, and had been cut and twisted while soft and then dried. With this slave whip in his hand he stood before the king's house and summoned him to come out.

The king put on his hat and came out. A more piteous man I think I never saw—a king, yet treated like a slave! The warriors accused him of spoiling all the rice, his own along with the rest, and told him that he was not fit to live among them, much less to be their king. I asked to be allowed to speak a few words, and they all sat down while I begged them not to give their king the "sasswood." If they wanted to banish him from their country that would be enough.

The Po River tribe are known as a very heartless people, and it is not an uncommon thing for them to put some of their number to death after a witch palaver or when anything else aroused their anger. They were eager to make another man king; and there was danger that they might take this opportunity to put Yaba out of the way by giving him "sasswood," and, in case the poison did not kill him at once, by knocking him down and breaking his neck with a mortar pestle. And then they would say that he had been put to death because he was a witch.

The people, however, declared they were not going to kill him, but, because of the harm he had done their country, that they intended to drive him away. They started him along the road to the beach, and they all followed him. Then they told him that he must take the beach road and leave their country, never to return. We waited in town at the king's house till the warriors came back and we knew that the king was gone; then we started home across the river, feeling that "the tender mercies of the wicked" were indeed cruel. Yet it was because of their darkness and ignorance that these people obeyed the devil-doctor; and they really believed that, somehow, good would come out of it.

The king started off up the beach, not knowing in what other direction to go or where to find a friend. The road led to another town of his own tribe; and before he had gone far he was met by a man who had come out to tell him to avoid the town for fear of his life. The poor king was terrified. His own people were both behind and before him. They were now his bitterest enemies. On the left the ocean barred escape, and a thick jungle lay on his right. Night was coming on; he was hungry and weary and had no covering or shelter against the long, chill hours of the morning. He stopped to consider. He was not willing to die, and had a horror—as all human beings have—of being put to death by the hand of man.

He turned aside into the jungle and sought a secluded place for the night, where he might be safe from his enemies. He sat down alone in the dark; and after the town had quieted down his son found him in his hiding place. As soon as day began to break the two made their way to the land of the Garraway people. They were received in a friendly manner by the king, and the son returned to his home, leaving his father with the Garraway king, who entertained him for ten months. During this time the son died, but Yaba was not allowed to go home to see him.

After his people thought he had been sufficiently punished for what he had done—he had really done nothing except try to rise a step above the condition of his fellows—they allowed him to come back to his own town, where he still remains, though he is held in great reproach among the people. The poor man is so crushed by his misfortunes that his only ambition is to get enough to eat and do as little as he can, that the envious people may not again rise up and devour all the fruit of his industry and economy.

His sons were very angry over their father's treatment, and their minds constantly brooded upon revenge. They used to say to me, "We no fit to forget this; when we are men we will do some of them so." And so the strife goes on, and nothing will stop it but the Gospel of love. Peace on earth and good will to men are the weapons with which to conquer these hearts and show them that there is a nobler life for them—one that, instead of filling the heart with bitterness, will fill it with love for their enemies and give to them a joy and satisfaction they have never found in returning evil for evil.

The people of Africa need many things. They are steeped in superstition, sin, and ignorance. A darkness that can be felt pervades the whole land. They live the lowest kind of life, and yet hope to reach some place of rest after death. All ye who know the love of God and the power of salvation, shrink not from obeying God's voice. Whatever work in his vineyard he has given you to do, do it with your might, that the light of the glorious Gospel of the Son of God, who is the joy of the whole earth, may shine into these dark hearts, and that they, too, may rise up and call him blessed.

CHAPTER VI.

BURYING THE DEAD.

Peculiar Manifestations of Sorrow.—Preparations for Burial.—Burying "Proper."—Gifts to the Dead.—Modes of Burial.—A Cemetery Rock in the Sea.—Nymer's Child.—Unwelcome Spirits.—Mourning for a Chief.—Communing with the Spirits.—Funerals without the Corpse.—Punishing a Dead Wizard.—Victims of Witchcraft.

ALTHOUGH the Africans wear charms to keep them from death, yet they die as surely as other people.

There are different modes of burial. No one dying a natural death is buried without, first, a great wailing and lamentation, and then a dance and rejoicing. As soon as a person dies a near relative—mother, sister, wife, or daughter—goes from house to house and from town to town wailing and crying and calling out the name of the dead. She does not stop to speak to anyone, but rushes on like mad, screaming at the top of her voice, throwing herself in the dust, and rolling on the ground; then up and away, paying no attention to anyone. She comes back finally to the corpse and throws herself down by it. And if any person touches her she is off for another frenzied round. She keeps this up for several hours, until she is too hoarse to speak above a whisper. Her friends and neighbors come in and sit around the corpse and cry, until they, too, are hoarse.

The body is washed, dressed, and laid on a mat in the center of the house. For the first day, especially if the death has occurred late in the day, there is a solemnity about the survivors that would indicate their deep sorrow at parting with their friend. They believe that the soul hovers around until the body is buried, and sees and hears all that is done.

After they have sufficiently mourned over the departed they prepare to bury the body. It is decked with beads, bracelets, and anklets. If it be that of an old person it is furnished with a pipe. A man has also a hat or cap placed on the mat at his head, and a woman has a comb put in her hair. A cloth is wrapped about the loins, and is sometimes changed every day until the corpse is buried. A number of posts are driven into the ground in the form of a summerhouse and covered with palm leaves, or sometimes with cloth. Boxes brought from the house form a bed, on which the corpse is laid with all the trinkets that adorn it. A waterpot stands near by with water for the frequent washing of the corpse. When the body is placed in the summerhouse the yard is dressed with tables, boxes, dishes, glassware, and pictures until it looks more like a variety store than anything else.

The dancing then begins; but the near relatives never join in the dance. If the deceased be a man his wives sit near him, the favorite wife at his head. They do not leave him until they are ready to take up the corpse and bury it. Then an old woman comes and takes the head wife by the hand and leads her away to a quiet place. She must not look around at her husband after she starts away. She is in mourning for a month or six months, as the case may be. She never puts on anything but an old blue cloth. Not until she has a new husband does she put off her mourning.

Two women died in our town, and we went to sympathize with the mourners, for they all expect this. They were not to be buried until the next day; but all the people were gathered there dancing. When any person dies all the town people are supposed to refrain from work out of respect to the deceased. One of the dead women had a son who had been down the coast several times, knew something about civilization, and wished to show the people that he could bury his mother "proper," as they say. He had a house for the corpse made of cloth, and had put up two lines on which he had spread out many yards of cloth, as if to prove how well provided for his mother had been. Poor woman! if she had had some of it while alive she might have lived more comfortably. Tables and boxes were set out with all kinds of trinkets. The corpse was dressed in the finest beads and anklets he could procure, and wrapped in a cloth of very good quality; and a pair of spectacles were put on her face—upside down. The people never wear glasses in life.

This dutiful son had supplied rum for the people, and they were all gathered at his place. The town women were dancing, singing, playing the *zah*, ringing bells, and laughing in great glee. They would carry the bell into the house, ring the bell over the head of the body, and dance around it. Then the leader would talk to the corpse and give it messages to deliver in the spirit world. The two dead women were not both in the same town; and after the people had gone through this performance in one town they would march over to the other town and go through it all again over the other woman. And so they spent the afternoon; and the night was spent in dancing and drinking.

Two goats were tied to the house ready to be killed in sacrifice the next day, together with some fowls. Human sacrifices are not now offered in Liberia; but it is common to kill a cow, and sometimes several, when any of the chief men die. When Paha died ten bullocks and several sheep and fowls were slaughtered. He was not a king, but a " big gentleman," and had the largest house in the tribe.

There are certain places set apart for burying grounds, which have been so used for years. Near every town is a place overgrown with low shrubs, where little children are buried. In another place grown people are buried; and in still another the kings and principal men.

In our tribe the bodies of certain classes of people are left on a rock out in the sea, near the mouth of the river. The people in general feel a horror at the thought of being buried in the ground, and desire to be laid away on the rock. It is the aristocratic burial place, and no one of notoriously bad character is taken there, nor any who cannot swim. They say that when the spirits meet for council only swimmers would be able to get away from the rock.

A sacrifice must be offered for all who are taken there. The coffin is carried to the top of the rock, and the corpse left to waste away in the sun. Rice and oil are placed near the coffin for the spirit to eat; and usually plates, cloth, powder kegs, boxes, brass kettles, jewelry, and other articles are placed by the corpse. In proportion as a person receives honor at his burial so, it is believed, will be his standing in the next world. All these articles—or the souls of them, for the natives attribute souls to all things—are the possessions of the dead in the spirit world.

How many times I have tried to persuade them from burying on this rock! And they are beginning to see that they ought not to do it. Since my return to America my sister, who takes my place at the mission, has written me the following experience of her own:

Garraway, May 16, 1895.

SISTER DEAR :

This has been a busy day. Yesterday morning a child died—Nymer's son—at the waterside town. After school I went and called on the family. This morning I heard that they were going to bury on the rock. So I went down and met Sampson, the king, and a lot of the chief men. I told them my errand. Wisser interpreted for me. Sampson heard me, and said that I must tell Kalenky and the other men.

When I told them Gray said, "No, we will bury on the rock. The first people did so, and we will do so too." Claba, Tie, Blay, Seere, Newey, and others, said it was their country fashion, and they were going to do as they had always done. I told them that it was not a good way to do; that they had been doing as the first people told them a long time; that they believed the devil-doctor, who had never done them good or told them when they were going to die; and that it was time for them to leave the old way. After some persuasion I said to Nymer, "Are you willing that your son shall be buried on the beach?" He said he was willing. I then asked if I might come and read and pray. Those there said, "Yes," and seemed glad.

I then came home. It was 9:30 A. M. I hurried the children who were cooking the breakfast, while I selected a reading for the occasion. Soon a man came for the shovel to dig the grave, and told me that they were going to do as I said and bury the child on the beach. A man was sent to tell me they were ready to bury the dead and that I must come. I took the children with me to help us sing. We first knelt and asked God to bless our efforts to show the people the true light.

When we got there they were not quite ready. They were finding some things to bury the boy with, and some of them were having dinner at Newey's place. The king sent me a plate of palm butter and rice, with some fish. I ate some of it. Then another man brought me some water to drink. They found seats for all the children and paid us every respect, even holding my umbrella over me while I ate.

When they were all ready they called me to read the Bible. They were very attentive to the end of the service. One of our young men interpreted for me. They had their own ceremony, and killed a goat and fowl. When they were ready two men took up the coffin and carried it quietly to the grave. They fired three guns in the town, and three more at the grave.

When I speak to the people so many times they say, "So teacher told us; we believe the word you and teacher say."

I am not lonely, but happy, blessed, busy, and joyful every day. Your sister twice,
JENNIE HUNT.

The Africans believe that the dead can come back again. If for any reason they have no desire to see a person again they insult him during his burial so that the spirit will never care to venture back. A woman who had already buried three children became the mother of twins; and they, too, died very young. When they were buried the family said that the same children had been coming back to the woman all the time, but would not stay. So the two were buried in one grave, and several shots were fired into it. This was done to discourage them from ever venturing back to this world.

Another child was born of a mother who had been very sick for some time before its birth, so that the child was a delicate little thing. It lived several months, but was always ailing; and when it died it was wrapped in a mat of rushes and buried. Heavy stones were thrown on its little corpse, and it was told that it was never wanted back in this world again.

Every tribe takes pride in having the grave of some chief located in a prominent place, and so decorated as to convey the idea that he has had great honor from his people.

In 1893 one of our chiefs died, and "was buried proper," as the people say. He was an old man, and the people, except his near relatives, were not sorry to see him die. They said that he had lived a long time and eaten "plenty good things," and that it was time he should go and give some other man a chance.

They buried him with great ceremony. A house was afterward built over the grave, with a fence around it; and on the fence were hung many yards of good cloth, holes being cut to make it useless so that the people would not steal it. Three umbrellas were stuck in the fence, and four hats. A rum barrel was set by the fence to show how much rum had been drunk in his honor at the funeral. Inside the fence were boxes, a table, and two good American chairs that his son had brought from sea, and spread out on these were looking-glasses, plates, bowls, basins, fancy dishes, and glasses of all kinds. On the pickets of the fence were eleven powder kegs, to show the quantity of powder fired off at his funeral.

At the time of the funeral the men dressed themselves in their war dress. Ever since the chief's death they had been dancing, drinking, firing guns, and having a good time generally,

BURYING THE DEAD.   109

such as they had not enjoyed for months. They painted themselves with clay, some red, some white; and some took pot-black and oil and made themselves blacker than they were born. All this was done to manifest their respect for the dead man—even to firing their guns at the coffin, until it was divested of the cloth with which it had been covered.

Three bullocks, several goats, and some chickens were killed for the deceased to take with him into the spirit world. All persons attending the funeral are supposed to bring a present to their departed friend. Dozens of plates, bowls, basins, and glasses, and many yards of cloth are given to the dead. But the family do not bury them all. They inform the dead man that they are his and give him a portion, but the rest are put away to be used for the survivors.

The third day after this chief was buried I was in the town, and I noticed that the women seemed anxiously looking for something. I inquired what they were searching for, and found that they were looking for a brass kettle. They said that the dead chief had come back and told them that in the land where he had gone there was no brass kettle for him to wash in, and he had come back to get one. The largest one in the town was brought out, a hole made in the bottom of it, and it was put on the grave with the rest of his possessions. A large silk flag was raised over the grave, and remained there until it was torn to tatters in the wind. This flag had been brought home from a sea voyage by his son, who had taken it in part pay for his work.

Quite frequently the kings and chiefs take a bottle of rum, go to this grave, light a fire, sit down and drink, and, as they say, consult the old chief in regard to the interests of the people. His share of the rum is poured on the top of his grave. It is a common thing for them to send messages to the devil and the spirits by this man. Especially in case of war or any serious trouble they put great dependence upon the devils and spirits.

In some tribes many persons are buried in one grave, the remains of earlier corpses being taken out and put on top of the new body.

Another strange custom prevails among them—that of "burying" those who die away from home or at sea. When the relatives hear of the death of their absent kinsman they mourn for him and go through the regular ceremony as best they can without the corpse. The rude coffin is made—a box four feet long being sometimes used to "bury" a man five feet in height! It is covered with cloth, and the usual offerings are made. But instead of being put in the earth, it is set up on a stand, made of poles, near the town. A small house or shelter is built over it, and all the offerings are hung on this house or laid on the top of the coffin.

In case of a person being put to death as a witch, by drinking a decoction of the deadly "sasswood" bark, there is no mourning. Even his near relatives rejoice that a bad person has been put out of the way; for they believe that a witch will harm his dearest friend. In such cases there is neither ceremony nor offering; but as soon as it is dead, and sometimes before it is really dead, the body is dragged out and thrown into the bushes, and a little mud is heaped over it to hide it from view.

I once saw them bury a young man who had died from the "sasswood" in this way. He died in the night and was at once buried by the people, who rejoiced that they had found out a witch and put an end to his crimes, which had culminated in the death of a man in the town. But after he was dead they feared that the disgrace heaped upon him and his family might cause him to take revenge. So women were sent into the woods where his spirit was supposed to be lingering, to lament for him and bring his spirit back to town again, that he might have a home among them. Otherwise they feared that when they went out to gather wood he might attack them and take revenge for the treatment he had received. I knew nothing of what was going on until I heard the women crying and saw them coming in a long line out of the bush. When I inquired what this meant I was told that they had been to the woods to bring back the spirit of the young man whom they had put to death.

The "bodier," or high priest, is never buried like other people. His body is taken away by a few men appointed to do so, and is buried at night under a stream of running water.

A young man who had gone to the bush to cut palm nuts was bitten by a snake. He died and received a common burial, and all the town mourned for him. But after the funeral the devil-doctor said that this young man had been a witch and had not deserved such respect. He had gone to the bush, not to get palm nuts, but to find "witch" with which to kill the king. The people were so enraged when they heard this that they went to the grave, took away everything they had placed there, brought their offerings back to town, and washed them. Then they took up the body and dug a hole in a swamp and buried it under water to show their contempt for the young man's memory because of what the devil-doctor had accused him.

These are but a few of the many awful things that are done among this people. And the spirit in which they are done is the most heathenish part of it all. In our own land, when a dear one has been called away, when the heart is sore with grief, and the world, with all it can give, does not fill the void that the departed friend has left, one's heart is softened and he is inclined to listen to the truth. Even the bystanders feel solemn when the funeral procession passes through the streets.

But, alas, how different is a funeral procession in Africa, especially if a person is supposed to have been witched! There is no hearse or wagon, not even a handcart, to bear the dead to the grave. Two men carry the coffin on their heads. If it be said that the departed has been the victim of witchcraft these men, after starting off in the direction of the grave, will turn and come back, sometimes running all over the town with the corpse still on their heads. Everyone stands by in fear to see what will happen; for they believe the spirit of the dead man has taken possession of the bearers.

When the two men come to a house they will stop and knock the coffin against it, start on again, and then go back to knock the coffin against the house a second time. As the houses are low it generally strikes the roof just over the door. The native house has two doors— one called the men's door, and the other the women's door. If the coffin stops before the men's door it is believed that the owner of the house is the one who has witched the deceased; if before the women's door, then the wife is the witch. After the person is thus formally accused of being a witch, the bearers continue their way to the grave and the body is buried.

I have noticed that the men always stop with the coffin at the house which the people have already decided among themselves to be the dwelling of the witch. Sometimes they take the accused out of the village and administer the poisonous "sasswood" drink. He lives or dies, according as his stomach is strong enough to throw it off or not. Our Christian young men are doing a great deal to destroy this custom, and often take up the coffin and carry it quietly to the grave and bury it.

The greatest power at work in Africa to-day to overturn these heathen customs and bring in a better day is the power of God; and according as we who know the light display it before them will the darkness disappear and the true light shine among them. The natives look to the white man for the better way and are accepting the light. Wherever I have gone among them, their one request was, "Can't you stay in our town? we want white man to be in our town;" and when I have told them that I could not leave my station, as I was alone and must do the work which had been given me, they have answered, "Well, can't you write to big America, and tell the white people we want them to come and live with us?"

"A call from a land where the beautiful light
   Is slow creeping o'er hilltop and vale,
Where broad is the field, and the harvest is white,
   But the reapers are wasted and pale.

"All wasted and pale with their wearisome toil,
   Still they pause not, that brave little band,
Though soon their low pillows will be the strange soil
   Of that distant and grave-dotted strand.

"There the strong man is bowed in his youth's golden prime,
   But cheerily sings at his toil;
For he thinks of the sheaves and the garnering time,
   Of the glorious Lord of the soil.

"But ever they turn, that brave little band,
   A long, wistful gaze toward the West.
Do they come, do they come, from the dear distant land—
   That land of the lovely and blest?

"Do they come, do they come? We are feeble and wan,
   We are passing like shadows away,
But the harvest is white—lo, yonder the dawn!
   For laborers, for laborers we pray."

CHAPTER VII.

NATIVE THEOLOGY AND MORALS.

Belief in a Supreme God.—Devil Worship.—Native Rest Days.—Their Treatment of Murderers.—How They Punish Marriage Infidelity.—Effectual Punishment of a Thief.—Talebearers.—Native Belief in the End of the World.—How the Moon Became Cold.—The Sky Will Fall.—Giving First Fruits to the Devil.

IN Rom. i, 19, we read, "Because that which may be known of God is manifest in them; for God hath showed it unto them."

To believe that there is a God who has made all things, who gives us life and takes life away, we do not need to be educated. The heathen, who have no conception of education or theology, who do not even know one written sign from another, who have no characters to represent ideas, are quite convinced of his existence, although they call him by as many different names as they speak languages. The natives of Liberia call God "Niswa." They believe he is ever near and sees them and knows all they are doing.

They always call upon him to witness when offering a sacrifice or judging a "palaver" (a dispute of any kind) or a trial. In case of trial by drinking "sasswood," the victim, before taking the poison, thus calls upon God, with eyes uplifted, to hear his solemn statement to the people: "God, thou knowest that I am not guilty. I have not committed this crime. Thou, who knowest the truth, knowest that I am not the guilty party; therefore I am not afraid to drink this 'sasswood.' I know that I might lie to these people and deceive them, but I could not deceive thee; and if I were guilty this 'sasswood' would kill me." Thus they drink it, not fearing the deadly poison, but believing that the all-seeing God will prove their innocence and make known the truth.

In case of sudden death or any terrifying calamity the heathen call upon the unseen God—Niswa—not upon their idols. The word of God truly says, "For God hath showed it unto them." I have come into direct contact with the heathen and have observed how much confidence they place in the Almighty God. Although in all their homes they have idols that they worship, and although all wear charms and trust in their *gree-grees*, yet when danger or trouble comes they look to him, believing that he alone can help them. This has given me new light on many passages in the Bible, and I have said of a truth, "God hath showed it unto them," for there was no other source whence they could have received such light and knowledge.

The heathen are not without law. They have no written statutes, no books to which they can refer to settle their disputes. Yet in many things they follow the laws which are found in the Bible; and the Ten Commandments, which are the foundation of law in all civilized nations, are practically acknowledged in many of the heathen customs.

The idol worshiper, or devil worshiper, believes that, if he should turn away from his idol to the true God, his devil would, out of jealousy, send some affliction or calamity upon him or his. He has the secret conviction that one God is all he ought to worship, which, however faulty in its application, is really an inkling of our first commandment—" Thou shalt have no other gods before me "—as well as of a clause in the second—" For I the Lord thy God am a jealous God." The word of God tells us that man has " changed the truth of God into a lie." These people once had the truth; and now the lie of devil worship has become one of the greatest hindrances to their receiving the Gospel. Almost without exception they will say, " God way is better. 'Tis true these *gree-grees* no do us better." But they are in constant fear of offending their false gods, and live a life of terror trying to please them, that they may escape the consequences which would follow their disobedience.

The third commandment forbids the taking of God's name "in vain." The heathen have great respect for their gods. Their idols are carefully handled, and their names spoken with a certain amount of reverence.

The fourth commandment relates to the day of rest to be kept holy unto the Lord. In the busiest time of the year the African heathen are to be found taking their rest on certain days. Sometimes I have gone to town and found the men, or perhaps the women, there, and have asked why they were not on the farm. "O," one would say, "I am tired; I am having a rest to-day." They do not all choose the same day, but rest on whatever day suits them best. Nobody ever thinks this custom wrong. But they oftener take the fourth or fifth day than the seventh. When we tell them that they ought to take the Lord's day they answer, "Yes, we fit to do that, for we all have a rest day." But the trouble is to get them to all keep Sunday together. Each thinks it all right if he keeps any day he chooses.

The natives do not have a day which they

keep holy unto their gods, except that whenever the devil-doctor sees fit to make a sacrifice to the devil or the gods he forbids the people to go to the farms or do any kind of work, sometimes not even allowing rice to be beaten for their meal or water to be brought; and the people show their reverence by leaving off their daily work. It might be said that they keep such days holy unto their gods, though not unto our God.

In our tribe a boy or girl who did not obey his parents was considered a bad child, and got many a beating for it. The heathen parent knows that his child should obey him, and expects the respect that God appointed when he said, " Honor thy father and thy mother."

The next law of Moses is that against murder. Murders are rare among the natives. In case of one person's accidentally causing another's death, the offender is banished and not allowed to return to his own people for a term of years—it may be five, seven, or ten. Often he never returns, having settled down by that time in another tribe. In such cases the stranger is kindly received, and often marries, learns the language, and becomes one of the new tribe.

If a person is known to have intentionally caused death he generally flees to another part of the country, fearing the vengeance of his own tribe if they should find him. If caught, there is no mercy for him. They sometimes give him "sasswood;" but if that does not kill him they knock him down with a pestle and then lay it across his neck, while a man jumps on either end and breaks his neck. Then they throw "sasswood" over him, and say the "sasswood" killed him. Sometimes they tie a large rock about the body of the guilty man, put him into a canoe, and take him far out to sea. Then they capsize the canoe, and he sinks to the bottom.

The Po River folk, who live across the river from our tribe, sent a number of their young men down the coast to work for the European traders. While there four of the young men died, and the survivors accused one of their number of having poisoned them. When their term of service was over and they returned home, the families of the deceased were so enraged at the accused young man that they met him in the boat as he landed, and, without trial, tying a rope round his waist, took him out into the river to drown him. Our tribe, who could see what they were doing from their own side of the river, rushed to the spot, took the young man from them, and saved his life.

These heathen, who have never been taught

from books that it is lawful and right for every man to "have his own wife" and every woman to "have her own husband," have in every tribe a severe law against adultery. While it is often broken, yet the breaker is liable to suffer the extreme penalty.

Shortly after I went to Garraway a man came to our house early in the morning, his face scratched and bleeding, and his eyes bloodshot from the sand that was still in them. He asked us to do something to relieve his pain, and we did what we could for him. Afterward we learned that he was suffering the penalty of breaking this law. In fear of the offended family he had fled to another tribe and spent some years there, hoping that the anger he had aroused would pass away. Then he had ventured home again. But members of the injured family, hearing that he was coming back, met him when he landed, gave him a severe beating, and rubbed sand in his face and eyes till he was in the pitiable condition in which he came to us.

A woman never receives more severe treatment at the hands of her husband than for the breaking of this law, often being burned with firebrands. They will rub her body with oil, stand her over a fire with a staff in her hand, and hold a blazing torch to her body. They say that unless she is guilty the fire will not burn her. If they are satisfied of her guilt they burn her severely—sometimes until she cannot rise from the ground. A man is sometimes so offended by this unfaithfulness that he will never live with the woman again, and will compel the offending man to take her and pay him money with which to buy himself a new wife.

The eighth commandment is recognized in every native town. But a few weeks before I left Garraway a woman had been found stealing vegetables from one of her neighbors, and the "Quee," which is a secret society of the men, undertook to execute the law in her case.

Soon after the town became quiet at night a company of these men, with drum, cymbal, and horns, went dancing and shouting past our house. They went to the town where the woman lived, marched into her house, and demanded a goat for their supper. The troubled husband caught the animal and gave it to them. Then they demanded rice. She had to give them all she had. Next they wanted her firewood, and she gave them all she had piled in her wood racks to dry for the rainy season. These articles they took and went away to prepare a meal to be eaten before morning.

But, wishing to beat the rice, they sent back for her mortar, and then for her fanner. They needed hot water to clean their meat thoroughly, and so sent to her for her pots, and then for her *glebbies* (rests to hold the pot over the fire). Soon they needed a knife, then some bowls, then salt and pepper for the soup. When all was ready they desired chairs to sit on, and rum to finish up the meal. All these things the woman or her husband or friends had to furnish, or it would have gone worse with them. By morning all that was left to the woman was the empty house. This was her punishment for having broken the law, " Thou shalt not steal ; " and nothing " Quee " demanded was ever returned. It is in this way that they suppress thieving.

The ninth commandment is against lying or bearing false witness. A liar is despised among them, although they do not always tell the truth. They have their notorious talebearers, who make the usual amount of trouble. Sometimes the accused, to prove his innocence, will drink "sasswood" or go through the trial of picking palm nuts out of boiling oil. In case his charges are proven false the talebearer often pays for his offense by having his house torn down or being compelled to give a bullock to the accused.

The man thus proved innocent will dress himself in all the finest trappings the tribe can produce out of their boxes and make the round of the towns singing his own praises and telling all the hateful things the talebearer has done and said, until he who has borne "false witness against his neighbor" is glad to make humble apologies for the untruths he has uttered and confess that he is in the wrong. By the time he gets the matter settled he has learned a serious lesson, which has, perhaps, cost him as much as if he had been in a court-room and settled it before a judge.

Covetousness is a curse to any people, and many deeds that blacken the homes of the Africans, as well as our own homes, spring from this sin.

The eleventh commandment, given by Jesus—"A new commandment I give unto you, that ye love one another"—is not found in heathen lands, and it is this want that makes the darkness in their homes and lives. "God is love." But the heathen do not worship God. This is the hardest thing of all for us missionaries to bear—the darkness with which we are surrounded. Jesus came to bring peace on earth and good will to men; but the heathen have no Jesus, no peace, and no light. The darkness can be felt. They are always at war one with the other; and the only way to better their condition is to preach Jesus to them. Let us all work to this end.

I had been in Africa four years before I learned that the native people had any idea that there would be an end to this world, or that everything would not always be as it had been. It was not until I learned the language and could understand them when they talked among themselves that I overheard the children talking about it.

One Sunday evening we were sitting on the veranda of our house. The moon was shining brightly. Many stars were visible in the sky, and the children were talking about them. I asked how big they thought the stars to be. They didn't know exactly—perhaps as big as their fists. I told them that they were as large, or far larger, than the earth on which we live. They could not understand how that could be, and were much interested in hearing about the heavenly bodies.

I asked them what they had been talking about, for I had just heard enough to make me curious. They replied that they had been told by their people that the sun and moon were both hot alike at first. But one day the sun and moon said, "Let us go and wash." They went down to the water; and the sun told the moon to plunge in first. So the moon got into the water and washed; and when it came out it was cold. Thereupon the sun refused to wash, for it did not wish to become cold. That is why the sun is hot and the moon is cold.

It was my turn to be interested now, and I begged for another story. They told me that their people said that the woodpeckers were cutting down the trees of the forest, the sandpipers counting the sands on the seashore, and the sea gulls drinking the ocean dry, and that some day woodpeckers, sandpipers, and sea gulls were all going to finish their tasks together, and that then the sky would fall.

I asked them who had told them this. Their fathers, they answered, and that, furthermore, when they heard the people converse about these things they were very much afraid. I told them that they need not fear, because God held the sky up, and it would not fall till he said so; but that God had said that some day this world should come to an end, and we must all be ready.

The next day I went to town and asked the people concerning these stories. They said they knew from their fathers that the sky was coming down some day. Some, however, did not believe it, for it was a long time since they heard the story and the sky had not come down yet. But the people generally do believe it, and I have often seen them during a thunderstorm beat the war drum, blow the war horn, and, sometimes, fire guns while the storm lasted. I asked why they did so, and was told that they were begging God not to let the sky come down upon them.

It is the law of God that man shall not consider all his earnings as his own, but shall give a part to his God. We read in the Bible that we are to give him the first fruits of all our enterprises. Some, in civilized lands, object to this giving and regard all they have as their own. They do not feel under any obligation to give to the cause of the God they profess to worship.

It is not so with the heathen in Liberia. I have often seen the people during the time of the rice harvest eating vegetables which they consider very inferior to rice, while at the same time they have the new rice in their houses. A native will not eat, or even taste, of the new rice until the harvest is all gathered. Then he will cook a pot of it, put oil upon it, or else kill a fowl and offer it in sacrifice to the devil whom he worships. He feels that he has no right to eat the first of the new rice which he has cut. So the first fruits are given to the devil, who is really his god. The young Africans, who are becoming more enlightened, do not feel it their duty to give the first to the devil, and some of them do not give him any at all.

If you watch a woman closely when she goes to dish up the rice for dinner you will see that after she puts the wooden spoon into the pot she takes some of the top of the rice in her fingers and places it on the floor for the devil's dinner.

Thus, all untaught, and in their poor, blind way, these poor Africans carry out the command of God, " Honor the Lord with thy substance, and with the first fruits of all thine increase." But their lord is the devil; and so, because they have " changed the truth of God into a lie," God is robbed of the honor due to him.

I have often noticed the old men taking snuff. One will take his snuffbox out of his hat, take a pinch of snuff out of it, then put his hand down by his side and drop a little on the floor before raising it to his nose. He was giving the devil the first of the snuff. His heart tells him that the first part of all he has does not belong to him, but to a higher power. I think that in this respect they might be an example to many a so-called Christian.

CHAPTER VIII.

INCIDENTS OF MISSIONARY LIFE.

An African Devil's Den.—Queer Furniture.—The Place where the Devil Smokes.—A Shameless Impostor.—Delicate Surgery.—Two Boys Struck by Lightning.—An Amateur Oculist.—The Kroo Mark.—A Garraway Enoch Arden.

ONE of the first things we learned when we reached Africa was that the people believe in a personal devil. God is "Niswa," and they say that he lives up in the sky; but the devil is quite a different person. He lives in this world and has many and various homes. Sometimes a certain piece of bush where heavy timber grows, generally on a hilltop, is called "the devil's home," and is not allowed to be used for any purpose.

We lived on the coast, and several of our towns were near the beach. At a certain place on the beach stood a very large rock. In it, on the side next the sea, was a cave where our people said that the devil lived. He had assumed the shape of a tiger. All the people lived in constant dread of this place. Not one of them could be induced to go near it except a certain devil-doctor, whose business it was to attend upon this devil; and he had taught them—and they thoroughly believed it—that if they should see the devil they would die.

Miss Binkley and I often asked where this rock was—there were several large rocks along the coast—saying that we wished to visit it. They told us that it was not safe to go there, and that even the chief men and the warriors never ventured near it, knowing that if they did they would never be seen again.

One day while visiting in the town we induced two of the young men to take us to the rock. They went with us until the rock could be seen, and pointed it out to us. "There is the cave," they said, "where his home is, and he is inside. No man can go and see him and live." But we said that we had never seen the devil, who did not live in the rocks in our country, and were determined to see him now. They were surprised that we were not afraid of such a place. They begged us not to go, assuring us that there really was a devil there, and that we would never come back. But we told them that we did not believe it. We had never heard of such a thing in "big America," and we were going to see if the devil really did live there. They did all they could to stop us.

But we started on alone, saying that we would tell the devil we were white women and had never seen him before. Surely he would not kill us just because we had come to see him. So we left the two men, who were in great fear lest this was the last time they should ever see us. For themselves nothing would induce them to go to such a place.

The tide being out, we walked along on the dry sand till we came to the rock. The mouth of the cave was not more than four feet high. We took off our hats and crawled inside. It was almost dark, for the only light that got in came from the small entrance, or sifted down through a crack in the top of the rock.

In the center of the cave we saw something that looked like a grave. At one end a stake about four feet high was stuck into the ground, and on the top of it was a strip of white cloth about a foot and a half long and two inches wide. Near this stake was a row of gin bottles. These the devil-doctor had taken there full of liquor for the devil, and after drinking most of it himself had given the devil the rest by pouring it out on the ground. He had then set the bottles halfway into the ground, to show how well he had treated his friend, the devil. There were twelve bottles in the row! On the ground lay a lot of decayed rice. This had been cooked and brought there for the devil to eat. A dismal place it was—cold and damp and dark.

After a thorough investigation we came out, and found the men where we had left them. They were much excited over our adventure. We told them that there was no devil in the cave, and that we thought that he must have gone away on some business or other, for we had talked loud, had looked the place well over, and knew that if he were there we should have seen him. We described to them what we had seen, and soon satisfied them that the devil-doctor was deceiving them.

We started back to town, and on the road came to a place where the grass had been cleaned away and a stake set up with several strips of cloth, such as we had seen in the cave, hanging on it; a pipe and some tobacco lay there, with several half-burned sticks, as if there had been a fire. The men said that this was where the devil came to light his pipe and smoke, and that the devil-doctor lit the fire and supplied everything he desired. The cloth was for the devil to wear. The piece was small, it was true, but he wore it in spirit and not in reality, and could make it as large as he liked, so that a little piece served his purpose as well as a big one.

We came back to town, but said little, for

we realized from the manner of the young men that it was no common thing we had done, and that they were fearful of what the people might do to them for showing us the way. Nothing happened, however, to make the people suppose that we had so insulted their devil as to visit him, the fears of the men wore away in consequence, and we began to speak of our having been to see the devil and not being able to find him.

One moonlight evening, when we were in town holding service, I spoke of the rock, and told the people that they feared the place without cause, because I had been there and had gone inside of the cave. I then described all that was there, and said that if any of them wished to see the cave I would gladly be their guide. I said that the devil-doctor had been telling them lies to frighten them; that they must not believe him; that the devil did not want a home in the rocks, but in their hearts.

Quite a crowd had gathered round me and had sat down in the sand. After the service I went about to shake hands with them, and there was Kiew, the devil-doctor, himself, among the rest. He had listened to it all without a word. I shook his hand and said, "You are the man that tells all the lies about the devil, and keeps these people in fear. And you know

A Trio of Witch Doctors.

it is not right. All those things you have given to the devil are wasted, and you know better." But he only laughed. He knew that I had been there, for he could see the tracks of my shoes; and as no other person at Garraway wore shoes he knew that I was speaking the truth.

Ever since the days of Jesus, who was the great Physician of both the bodies and souls of men, and went about laying his hands on the sick, ministering to the suffering, and urging the ungodly to repent and be converted, have people expected to see his followers do the same. The life of Christ was the example of the Church, and wherever she enters the suffering flock to her for relief.

I believe every missionary of the cross in heathen lands, as well as at home, has a long story to tell of the physical sufferings they have been called to relieve. The people expect them not only to preach salvation for their souls, but to give them some healing for their bodies. This is one of the first things that impressed me in Africa. The natives had not been told that I had any medicines, but naturally thought that I would understand all their pains and aches and be able to give them relief.

In a civilized land, where doctors and nurses

are easily found, it is not the minister's work to care for the sick and dress the wounds of the unfortunate. But in Africa, where there are no capable doctors and where the people know so little about surgery, I often felt it my duty to do what I could for the suffering, knowing that there was no one else who would do more for them or understand their cases better.

Cuts are very common among the natives. I have had numerous cases of the sort to attend to, and have had considerable success in treating them. One of the king's sons, who had gone to the rice farm with his mother, went off to play with some other boys while she was weeding the rice. He climbed a slanting tree, but fell, striking a stake below and cutting a gash in his abdomen three inches long. The intestines protruded, and the people were much alarmed, fearing that there was no hope for the boy.

They brought him at once to the mission house, and laid him down on the ground outside. We were busy in school, and did not see them until one of the men came to the door and spoke. They called me outside. I went and saw the boy. He lay on the grass quite exhausted.

They told me what was the matter. I felt

very timid about doing anything in a case of the kind. There was no one, however, who could do any better, and the father begged me to do what I could, promising, in case I cured his boy, to allow him to remain always in school. He looked upon his son as dead, knowing that the case was quite beyond the skill of his people.

I appointed one of the older boys in the school to teach the rest, and then went to work. With a soft cloth and lukewarm water I got the intestines back into place. I sewed up the wound with a common needle and thread, applied arnica, and bandaged it well. Then I brought him into the house and laid him on his back. He stayed with us, and with rest and good nursing it was not many weeks before he was well again. The native way would have been to keep the wound open, and bathe it several times a day in hot water. This, of course, would have been very dangerous, for soon there would have been a badly inflamed sore, with probably fatal results. I have found the people very poor doctors in treating wounds and cuts, though in treating some other things they do very well.

One day, in a heavy thunderstorm, two of our mission lads were stunned by lightning. They were in the house at the time, and were both felled to the floor. One of our missionaries happened to be present, and together we picked them up, carried them out into the yard, and began to bathe them with cold water. Neither of us had had any experience with such accidents before, and I feared that perhaps we were not doing the best thing possible. So I ran and looked in the doctor's book. The directions were: "Put the patient on fresh ground, turning the face to the west, and then bathe well with cold water." I ran back, and we continued to bathe the boys until the pain was gone and they could stand on their feet again.

By this time quite a crowd had gathered. I asked them, "Now, if this had been in town, what would you have done?" They replied, "Our people dig a hole in the ground, put the person in the hole, cover him up to the neck with dirt, and then pour water on him." I told them that that was about what I had read in the book, and that I believed they knew a good deal more than they thought they did. Our American doctors, who had spent many years going to school to learn these things, said this was the right thing to do.

At another time some of our boys went to gather shells off the rocks out in the sea. While knocking these shells off a rock, one of the boys struck a kind of jellyfish, some of which spurted in his eye. He did not say much when he came home that day; but the next morning his eye was swollen and red. He told me that this was a very bad thing to get into the eye, as it would sometimes cause the eyeball to burst.

I went to the doctor's book to learn what to do. The book said that in many cases one of the best things for the eye was spittle. It added that, although some physicians were too polite to spit in the eye of a patient, but would prescribe some preparation not half so good, yet saliva was often best.

I thought this a very simple remedy for so serious a case, for the boy seemed really in danger of losing his sight. I thought that his mother might perhaps know of something that would be better; so I sent him to town to see whether he could not get relief from some one who understood the working of this poison. He soon came back with three palm nuts in his hand. I asked him what his mother said. He answered that she had chewed up a palm nut, then spat it all out and spat in his eye. She had given him these three palm nuts and told him to have somebody do the same thing for him two or three times a day. I did so, and his eye was soon well.

These things showed me that knowledge is not all confined to the learned, and that in some things the heathen are as well posted as the civilized and educated.

The people on the coast of Liberia have an ancient custom of putting a mark on the middle of the forehead. It is not for decoration, as similar marks are with many heathen peoples. Among uncivilized peoples who wear no clothes it is a very general custom to tattoo their bodies. Some of our African people, indeed—especially those who are not very black and on whom the marks show well—have their bodies elaborately decorated; and some of our young men who have worked for Europeans and received an English name have this name tattooed upon their chests.

But the mark on the forehead is known by all the European traders as the "Kroo" mark, and when they find a man with this mark they know he is from the Kroo coast. This custom has grown out of slavery, and is a sign that these people are not slaves, but free, and were born in a free country.

This indelible mark is made in early childhood, by cutting several small gashes with a knife in the skin until it bleeds well, and then rubbing into it a mixture of oil and pot soot. When it heals it is black and cannot be washed off. I think it a very good thing in that land where slavery is so common and where the people mix with all kinds of strangers; and it has been the means of saving some of them from being carried away into slavery.

Some time before I arrived at Garraway a number of these Kroo boys had gone down the coast to work. One of them, named Tubbah, had been sent in a surfboat with some other boys to a distant place. While on their way they got into a quarrel, and the others threatened the life of this young man. Having none to befriend him, he jumped into the sea and swam ashore; and the people on the beach seized him and sold him to a slaveholder in the far interior.

His wife and friends at Garraway waited anxiously for some word from him, but heard nothing, until after several years they gave up all hopes of ever seeing him again and mourned for him as dead. His wife was given to another man.

After six years had passed word came home that Tubbah was still alive and would soon return. His master had kept him away from the coast all these years, fearing lest he should be recognized by his Kroo mark. But at this time he had to come down for some purpose and thought it would be safe to bring Tubbah along.

While they were on the coast an English gentleman saw him and asked him where he came from, who he was, and how he came to be there with that mark upon his face. Tubbah told his story. The Englishman then sent for his master and told him that he could not take a free man home with him, that Tubbah was his own Kroo boy and he knew where his home was, and was going to take him to his own people. The master could make no reply, for he knew that he had enslaved a free man.

So the Englishman kept Tubbah and sent him home to Garraway by the next steamer. I saw him as he walked up the little road that went past our house into the town, with the people crowding around to welcome him home again. He spent several days among them. Soon he learned that his wife had been given to another man and was living in another town twenty miles distant.

After a short time he went to see her. It is not a custom in Africa to rap on the door before entering, but, without an invitation, the visitor walks in and sits down. Tubbah found the house of his wife and walked in and sat down. She and her present husband were astonished to see one whom they had believed to be dead; but Tubbah was very pleasant, and thanked the man for being kind to his wife and taking care of her for him during his absence. Then he turned to his wife and said, " Dwady, I have come for you. Come on and let us go home."

She was quite cross with him at first, and acted as if very much vexed at her old husband for coming after her. But in a few days she said to her second husband, " Well, I have made up my mind to go back to Tubbah, and I shall have to say good-bye to you."

So she took her son and started off to her old husband.

Tubbah, of course, was very glad and the other man very sorry, for he had but one wife. He urged her to stay; but she said she must go. " Is it possible," he said, " my good wife is going to leave me?" and sat down and cried when she departed. I have visited Tubbah and his wife since they commenced keeping house again. They are living very happily in one of our towns.

CHAPTER IX.

VISITING NEIGHBORING TRIBES.

Visit to the Po River People.—First Ride in a Canoe.—
"Yem Plu Deen E Oh."—A Talkative Meeting.—A
Trying Night.—Up River to Peddie.—Caught in the
Rain.—Peter's Conversion.

THE tribe nearest to us was the Po River people.

Every tribe of any size is divided into two sections, living several miles apart. This is done that they may be better able to control their land and may more easily attend to their farming. If they all lived in one place some would be obliged to go too great a distance to their plantations.

The Po River tribe occupied a long, narrow tract of land on the coast. The principal towns, where the king lived, were fifteen miles up the coast. The smaller part of the tribe lived in three towns, just across the river, and within plain sight of our house.

We had been in Garraway but a short time when several young men who were anxious to accept Christianity and attend the school went with us one Sunday morning to hold service in the towns across the river. We were a company of thirty, and all had to cross in a canoe.

It was my first canoe ride, and I confess that I felt a little shaky. As the sand was all wet one of the men took me in his arms, carried me to the canoe, and set me down on a small box they had brought for me to sit on.

At every move I made the canoe tipped threateningly; but when a number of the others got in they were so much at home there that their confidence gave me courage, and I began to breathe more easily. The canoe was of medium size—about two feet in breadth and twenty feet long. After we had crossed one of the party paddled back for the rest.

When they were all over we started for the town. We marched along one after the other, and as all the young men were dressed in their best clothes they looked quite respectable to my eyes. It was very encouraging to notice the difference between them and their almost naked fellows we had left behind us.

As we neared the town the people came out to see who were coming. They had seen some of their own young men dressed in civilized clothing; and, since they knew all the young men who were with me, they were not so much surprised at their appearance. They knew, moreover, that there were white women at the mission in Garraway, for many of the Po River men had been to call on us. So now their first thought was that these young men were bringing one of the white women over to see them.

When they discovered me among the rest they began to call out, "Yem plu deen e oh! Yem plu deen e oh! Koo deen e oh! Koo deen e oh!" The word "koo" is their word for both "devil" and "white people." When they first saw a white person they thought it was the devil or a spirit, and so they call the white people "koo." They also call us "yem plu," meaning "white man."

Soon every person in the town heard the cry and came out to see the great sight, for no white woman had ever been there before. But few of the people, outside of the young men, had ever seen a white person. Many of the women, as soon as they saw I was white, ran away and kept at a safe distance until I was gone. Some of the women and all the men came and shook hands with me and were quite friendly. But the children were all afraid, and many of them ran crying to their mothers, and remained in terror until I left the town.

An old blind woman came out of her little hut as I passed by and asked to put her hands on me. She felt my hands and face, my hair, and all my clothes, and then said, "I see something I never see before." She told those standing by that she had never expected to live to meet a white person, and that God had been good to let her live to see that day. After a good meeting in the three towns we returned to Garraway.

I had taken a lunch with me, for I knew I should not be home in time for a noon dinner. We crossed over to our side of the river, and while the young men were gone to get their lunch I sat down under a tree to eat mine. Soon we were ready for a service among our own people. We held three services in the towns, the young men helping along very well. They all sang, while some prayed and spoke.

At another time I visited the other towns of the Po River people. The king's son had urged me to go, and said that he would take me. That meant only that he would go with me, for I should be compelled to walk all the way. The towns were fifteen miles away, with one village about the middle of the journey.

We started about eight o'clock in the morning, and at half past ten we reached the halfway place. The king, an old man, was there and glad to meet me, and at once set to work to get a meal ready for us. This is characteristic of the natives of Liberia. They know that traveling is difficult, and expect a traveler to be hungry, and so, without saying anything, they provide something to eat.

I was very thirsty, for we had walked in the hot sun along the sandy beach. They gave me water, but it was very bad, and after I had swallowed it I turned very sick. They furnished me with a mat and a blanket to make a bed with, and a stick of wood, such as they use for a pillow.

They had a small house, intended for strangers. It took the place of the spare bedroom in one of our American houses very well. It was built of the native materials, but was set on posts two feet above the ground, and had a floor of platted bamboo. Here I lay down and had a rest and something to eat. This house was much the most comfortable in the town, since there was no fire in it. But the door was very small, and so low that I had to bend almost double to get inside.

About two o'clock we started on up the coast to the big town. The road seemed long, for I was weak and the sun was hot. I should hardly have arrived before dark had not the king's son allowed me to take his arm so as to help me along. When we reached the town the people were out on the farms, and we rested until they returned. A few of the old people and some women had been left at home, but they were not numerous enough to be tiresome.

But when the people came home there was tremendous excitement among them at seeing a white person in town! They had never seen the like before. They crowded around, talking at the top of their voices—some afraid, others crowding so close that it was not at all comfortable on so warm a day.

At dinner time they placed before us great plates of palm butter, rice, and fish. Several of the people had killed fowl, and each felt that I must eat some of the food which he had brought. Of course I could eat very little of what was set before me, for each plate contained much more than enough for a whole meal, but I had to taste it all. One of them would say, "Now, I am going to eat what is left, and by and by I shall be white too!" One of the women standing by said, "Give me the water left in the glass you have been drinking out of. I will drink it, and it will cause me to have a white child!"

After dinner I started to hold a meeting. I had brought one of my boys along, and we two began to sing. The people were much interested and listened well, but as soon as we stopped singing and I began to talk they all began to talk too, and it was impossible to be heard. They all talked at once, and made so much noise that we sang again to get them to be quiet.

But there were so many of them, and they were so very unruly, that even the king's son could not get a hearing for himself, or be heard when he interpreted what I said. It was so dark that I did not have a chance to read. We tried twice to get away from the crowd, thinking that perhaps we should be able to do better if we did not have so many around; but they all followed.

I was tired out with my day's walk, and my head was aching from the terrible noise; so I inquired where I should sleep, and they said, "In the king's house." I told them that I was going to bed, since they would not listen to what I wanted to tell them. Then they begged me not to go, saying that there were some who would like to hear, if the rest would only keep quiet.

I went into the king's house, and a few followed me. I asked them to shut the door and not let the rest enter. They shut the door, but those outside kept knocking at it until it had to be opened to let some of them in. Then others would come, and they also had to be let in, so long as there was any room.

Those in the house begged me to talk to them. We had no lamp, our only light coming from the fire that burned at one side of the room. We all sat down on the floor, and for an hour and a half I talked to them, until I was so tired I could not tell another story. I then told them to go out and let me go to sleep. But they would not go as long as I was to be seen.

Some of the young men went to work to fix me up a bed. They knew, somehow, that white people did not sleep on the floor. They found a few pieces of plank that had been nailed together in the shape of a door about four feet long. These they brought in and put down not far from the fire, blocking them up from the floor about four inches. Over them they placed a mat; and the king brought out his old coat, that had served many years and was almost stiff with dirt and grease. He suggested that this would make a good pillow. It was folded up and laid on one end. A blanket was found for a covering, and the bed was ready.

I said nothing, for I did not think that they would be likely to make it any better. So I spread my handkerchief over the old coat and lay down, dressed as I was. I lay very still for a time, in hope they might come to the conclusion that I was asleep, and be induced to go out and let the house cool off, for it was late, and I knew I should not get much rest if the fire was not soon allowed to die out. The natives do not like to sleep without a fire for a light; but when they all fall asleep it gets a chance to go down somewhat, until some member of the family gets up and feeds it again.

Soon the people went to bed. But I was very uncomfortable. My pillow was abominable. I pushed it aside and put in its stead a stick of wood that was lying near. There was a bunch of palm nuts on the floor about four yards from my head. These the rats were nibbling most of the night. I drove them away several times, but there was a large family of them, and they were bound to have their share of the nuts.

The mosquitoes were most unmerciful, notwithstanding the house was full of smoke. Moreover, the bedstead was several inches too short at both ends. I tried in vain to find a comfortable position, and as it drew near morning I had not yet had even a short nap. I drew the mat off the bedstead they had fixed up for me, and lay down on the floor with the rest of the people, for they all seemed to be more comfortable than I.

The chickens on the roost at the far side of the fire gave the alarm when it was time to rise. I rose quickly, took some water in a cup, and went outside to wash my face. I poured a little of the water into my hand, dashed it over my face, wiped my face with my handkerchief, combed up my hair, and started out to see the town. A crowd of the people again gathered around me, but they were more ready to listen than in the evening; and we had a good meeting.

After breakfast we started for home, and found the people of the middle town waiting for us. They had all stayed at home from the fields that day to see me when I passed. We had dinner and some cocoanut water there, and a good meeting; and we went on to the mission feeling that there was no place like home.

At certain seasons of the year our people are accustomed to catch a quantity of fish in the river with a drift net; and our mission boys were anxious to learn the art, that they, too, might get some fresh fish. I knew it would be a good thing for us, and would be a great help toward providing for the house.

So I took two of the boys one day and

started in a canoe up the river to Peddie, to buy a net; for the Peddies made these nets and our people did not. We started early in the afternoon, knowing that it was not many miles and that we ought to be able to get there inside of two hours if all went well.

One of the boys had been to Peddie and thought he knew the way. And he did know the one they formerly used. We followed this old route for some distance, until we came to a tree lying across the river. There was no way to pass around it. We shoved up alongside and got out on the log while the boys lifted the canoe over the obstruction. Then we got in again and pulled on up the river.

It had rained in the morning and was threatening when we left home; and now the rain began to fall. Soon we came to another fallen tree. This one was very large, and we did not know what to do. We were all wet from the rain and much water had come into the canoe, so that we were very uncomfortable.

We looked around, and near the edge of the river we saw a large limb that we thought might be cut off to permit the passage of the canoe. I got out and stood on the log while the two boys with a cutlass hewed off the limb. We had no ax and the cutlass was very small—somewhat like a large knife.

The boys got the canoe through under the log while I stood upon it and shivered in the rain. We started on again, but found signs that the road had not been used for some time. We worked our way through the overhanging bushes, and soon came to another small log. This we clambered over without cutting and shoved our way on toward the town, fearing lest we should have to stay in the bush overnight; for it was getting toward evening.

But just before dark we came near to the town. The place where we landed was not the regular landing place, but it was the best place for those coming by the old road. We were as wet as could be with sitting in the uncovered canoe. The place was a swamp. The boys were too cold and tired to do much to help me; but we heard some one in the bushes, who came when we called to him and carried me through the mud and water until we reached a path that led to the town.

This man took us to the king's house, which was warm and dry, though full of smoke. I was so very wet and cold that I feared a chill if I sat in my wet clothes. The king kindly got me a blanket to wrap around myself, and I took off my wet clothes and hung them up to dry. I took off my shoes, also, and set them by the fire.

The king's wife got supper and the people gathered in, and we had quite a meeting. I had taken no book this time, for we had hoped to be home again that night; but there was a young man present who had an English Prayer Book, which they brought to me. Another man had a picture of Jesus Christ on the cross. With the help of these we read and explained to them the plan of salvation and talked of the things of God until it was late. Some men brought in a few fathoms of fish net, and this we bought to take back with us.

The people finally went out, and I retired. A mat made of the leaves of the pah tree, with a stick of wood for a pillow and a cloth for a covering, was my bed, and was placed on the mud floor of the hut. After I had gone to bed a number of men came from another town with more net to sell. I got up and bought it; and in the morning we were ready to start back home.

I called on a number of the people before breakfast was ready, talked to them of the things of God, and held a short meeting; and then started for home. There was so much water in the road that my feet were thoroughly wet before we got started down the river; and it rained quite heavily all the way. When we reached our own town the people gathered round me and shook hands with me, glad to see me home and expressing their sorrow at seeing me so wet.

When I started from the town for the mission house our children saw me and came running down the hill to meet me. Bestman had kept house for me, and he was with the rest. If I had been away six months they could not have made more ado over my coming home.

I was very thankful not to be seriously sick after my exposure. I did, indeed, have a little fever—just enough to tell me that it is not a good thing in Africa to get wet.

The Sunday following the young men and boys went early to Po River to hold a meeting in the town before the people should get away in the morning. Peter, my oldest boy—nineteen years of age—was left home to cook the breakfast. After their return we all sat down for our morning meeting; but Peter was missing. He had been much concerned about his salvation, and we had all been praying God to save him. Some of the boys said that he had gone to the bush. So we went on with the meeting without him. We had not been long started when we heard some one coming up the walk clapping his hands and saying, "My soul is happy! My soul is happy! Jesus has washed my sins away. My soul is happy now." Peter came running into the house and shook hands with me, saying, "Teacher, Jesus has washed my sins away to-day!" He shook hands with several in the meeting, and talked to us of what Jesus had done for him.

We all knelt down and prayed and went on with our meeting. The event made quite a stir among us, as none present had ever before seen a person converted. Peter was soundly converted that morning, as his after life showed. He had been so miserable and anxious about his soul that he had gone to the bush to pray, and it was there that he found Jesus.

What a joy to the Christian that Jesus will receive any sinner at any time, in any place, even in the midst of an African forest! How I have rejoiced as I have seen my dear boys and girls get hold on God and experience his saving power! They are just as much changed as any other sinner when the power of God transforms their hearts.

What a wonderful and Almighty Saviour we have, that he can make himself understood to those in heathen darkness! Wherever there is a heart that sincerely seeks him it does find him. There are already a few native people that know for themselves that God has power on earth to forgive sins. But O what a host there are still who "sit in heathen darkness."

CHAPTER X.

IN JOURNEYINGS OFT.

Missionary Journey up the Coast.—A Missing Trader.—Becalmed in a Fog.—Christmas at Cape Palmas.—Another Helper at Garraway.—Up the Cavalla River.—A Woman Put to the " Sasswood."—Falls of the Cavalla.—Runaway Wives.

ON the first of December, 1890, our agent at Cape Palmas and Miss Dingman, one of our missionaries, came to our station at Garraway, on their way up the coast on business. I had not yet visited any of the coast stations, and therefore went with them to see the work at other points. We had a fair wind, and reached Sasstown at seven in the evening, a distance of seventy miles—an unusually quick trip. As we never have daylight at seven o'clock in Liberia, it was quite dark when we reached the town.

We landed from the surfboat which had brought us, and procured a lantern and some men to go with us to the mission, a distance of about two miles. There had been rain, and water lay in the little footpath. Sometimes we waded through mud; and when it got too bad the men carried us over the worst pools. We reached the mission at last, thoroughly wet from the rain and the walk in the long grass along the road. After drying ourselves and having supper we retired for the night.

The next morning we went out to see the mission grounds, and the little town of native Christians who had been converted and moved out of the heathen town. They are living civilized lives, and look like persons clothed and in their right mind.

After a pleasant visit at Sasstown we started back down the coast to Piquininni Sess. There is a mission house there; but it had been closed for some time, and we could not stay there all night. We went, therefore, to the native town, where we were quartered in a native house owned by one of the traders.

The traders did all they could to accommodate us, and provided us with a good supper of palm butter and rice. There were no beds, but they got planks for Miss Dingman and myself to lie on. We lay down, but could not sleep. The smell of the palm kernels, palm oil, tobacco, salt fish, and other articles of trade was so strong, and the people kept up so much noise, that, putting it altogether, we could not sleep at all.

The boat was loaded in the night with the produce the traders had collected to send to the Cape, and before sunrise we started, glad to get away safely; for there seemed to be some danger of there being trouble before we left. It was for this reason the boat was loaded and we left before daylight. The tribe around the station is known as a very hard people to get along with. The mission is now (1895) occupied by a young native man and his wife; and he writes me that he is succeeding nicely, and that God is blessing his work.

Grand Sess, the next station, was five miles down the coast. We arrived there in time for breakfast. Mr. Robertson, the missionary, who has been there since February, 1889, entertained us well. His Christian people came in to see us, and we had quite a house full. Brother Robertson, who does not miss an opportunity to sow the good seed, called a meeting then and there, and we all spoke and enjoyed the service.

Although rain had been falling and it was very damp, yet, as we were anxious to get home, we started for Garraway, twenty miles farther down the coast. There was no wind, and our boatmen rowed for several miles until they were tired. Then they let the oars rest for a while. Seeing, however, that we were not likely to reach home that way, they took hold and rowed again.

About halfway down to Garraway we stopped to wait for a trader whom we expected to pick up there. When on our way up the coast we had met with some of the Wet Harbor people out fishing in the sea. They came up to our boat and demanded tobacco. They said they were willing to buy it. No trader had been to their town for some time, and they had quantities of palm kernels. If anybody would bring tobacco ashore they would buy it all that day. Accordingly, a trader in our boat, seeing that there was no other way of getting rid of them, took a sack of tobacco and got into their canoe to go ashore and buy the kernels.

He made an arrangement with the captain of our boat to stop for him on the way back. We waited for him a short time. But there was a heavy mist, and we feared that he would not see us; yet as the landing was bad the captain did not venture in very close. After waiting awhile and seeing nothing of the trader we started on.

The men rowed on and on, and we shivered in the cold rain. The mist was so thick that the captain could not tell where he was. It grew very dark, and there we sat becalmed. They had taken down the sail, and were depending on their own strength to reach a landing.

The hours rolled on. None of us had a timepiece with us, to tell us just how late it was. Those of us who had brought watches to Africa had laid them aside before this, for they had stopped and were therefore useless, as there was no one to clean or repair them. Still, we knew it was getting late or, perhaps, early in the morning.

Some of the boatmen went to the bow of the boat, and declared, judging by the rocks they could see, that we were off Fishtown, ten miles beyond Garraway, where we wished to land. After some discussion the captain went forward to the lookout. He said we were not at Fishtown, but at one of our own towns, and that we were about a mile past the mouth of the river where the landing was. So they turned the boat around and pulled back, and we got ashore. It was half past two in the morning when we got home to the mission house ; and after getting some supper we all retired for the night.

Arrangements were made at this time for all the missionaries to meet at the Cape, with their school children, to have a Christmas entertainment. It was thought that it would be a good thing for the work, and a means of refreshing to the workers, to meet together and have the privilege of exchanging ideas. It was also felt that it would be a help to our children to meet with others of their own age who were clothed in civilized fashion, and who were in school for the purpose of learning something unknown to their fathers.

I at once set to work to get our children ready, which was not a small undertaking, for we were now twenty-four in number—men, women, children, and a baby. Miss Dingman remained with me at Garraway to help us get ready; and on the day before Christmas we left for the Cape.

As the weather was bad and we were going by boat the captain said we must start before day. So we were ready and embarked at three o'clock in the morning. At daybreak it began to storm, and we were out in a drenching rain until three o'clock in the afternoon, when we reached Cape Palmas, dripping wet. The children had shivered in the rain all day, and not one of them had a dry garment to put on.

The entertainment was to be that evening. So after supper we all went over to the church. The workers had arranged a beautiful Christmas tree. Every child had a present on it. We spent a very pleasant evening together, and the children were more than delighted.

The next day was Christmas, and the children from the different stations had an enjoyable day together, and a very good dinner.

On the twenty-sixth three couples from our tribe were married—Bo and Mannah, Dee and Cano, Doo and Wisedday. They had been man and wife before, but had forsaken heathenism and wished to be married according to God's law. One of our missionaries married them in the church.

We remained over Sunday and attended the service with the other missionaries. On Monday morning we left for our home. All had enjoyed Christmas very much, but I was glad to get my flock all safely home.

In February of 1891 Mrs. Minor and her son Johnny, a lad of eleven years, came out to help me with the work at Garraway. For the first six weeks they enjoyed it. They liked the country and the work, and we lived very happy together. Then Johnny was taken sick, and soon Mrs. Minor was taken down with the fever. For two days and nights she was unconscious. I feared she would not get better. The little boy was sick in bed, and I spent some anxious days.

It was decided that the best thing to do was to send word to the Cape and see if any relief could be obtained for the sufferers. A boat was accordingly sent up from the Cape with a Liberian woman on board, bringing word from our agent that if Mrs. Minor cared to come to the Cape the boat would take her down. There she would receive better care, and more appetizing nourishment could be had for her than in Garraway.

Both invalids were somewhat better, but thought it best to go. I got their things ready, and they started, in hopes of getting well and being able to return to the work. After they reached the Cape they steadily improved; but it was not long before Mrs. Minor wrote for the things she had left, saying that she would not return to Garraway. She had changed her mind, and would take up some other work.

The day I received this letter was the most lonely day I have had in Africa. "Is it possible," thought I, "that I am alone again?" The family was large, and the sewing, teaching, services, and superintendency of all the work, both in the house and on the farm, seemed enough to crush me, and I could not keep the tears back all day.

I had always kept close to my work, and, with the exception of my single trip up the coast, had not visited any of the other stations. Some of the missionaries, however, desired to go up the Cavalla River to visit the stations there; and I thought it would be a good chance to go. So I took four of our Christian men and went with the rest.

We were a company of twenty-two. Starting out in the morning, we walked most of the way in the hot sun, along the rough roads, through the bush, over many logs and roots of trees, and past the rice farms. We were carried over the water in a hammock. About four o'clock in the afternoon we came to Barraky, where Miss White and her sister are stationed. We remained there over Sunday and had good meetings, first in the town and then in the mission house. We had a good day, and all rejoiced in the presence of God among us, and the interest the people took in the services.

On Monday morning we started for the river. At three o'clock we reached our destination. Some of us visited the Episcopal mission on the river, and went from there to a neighboring native town.

We were all very hungry, but got some *cassadas* and roasted them until the dinner was cooked. When the people came in from their rice farms they gathered around us, and we talked to them of the truths of God. Many were very much interested, and seemed to understand that the truth of God would be a benefit to them and that God's law was right.

As we knew that we must sleep in the native towns we had brought blankets with us. These we spread on the mud floor of the house and, with a stick of wood for a pillow, lay down for the night. But I did not sleep, and never have been able to sleep lying on a mud floor, which always seems to me harder and more uncomfortable than lying on a plank.

In the morning we started up the river in two canoes. After several hours' pulling we reached Wissika station, where we met Hugo Hoppie and his wife, who were in charge.

After having lunch there we went on several miles farther to Eubloky station, which is in charge of Mrs. Tubman, a good Liberian sister. She had a house full of little adopted boys and girls in her school. We stayed here all night and had a pleasant time with the family, but saw very little of the townspeople, as the mission is at considerable distance from the village.

In the morning we went on our way to Yahky, which was then in charge of Miss Bates, who has since married Mr. Walker. Here we had dinner, and then continued on to Tataka, several miles farther. Here we made our headquarters, with Miss Whitfield, the missionary in charge.

We intended going on up the river to the falls the next day, but could not get a guide. As we would not be able to find our way alone we were obliged to wait a day. The next day we started up the river, intending to get our guide as we went along.

When we came to the town where he lived we found everybody greatly excited. A man had died, and they had caught a woman and were going to give her "sasswood;" for they said that she was a witch and had been the cause of the man's death. We found that they had already taken her a little distance out of the village to drink the "sasswood." We were obliged to wait until we found our guide; and while doing so several of us started out to see if we could not possibly save the poor woman from the ordeal.

On the way some men stopped us, and, standing in the path, asked us, "What side you live go?" "To see them woman," said we.

"No; you no fit," said they.

"How? We no come for palaver."

"O, but you go heave them 'sasswood' out," they said.

We told them that we were not going to

throw away the "sasswood" but wanted to see what they were doing. So they let us pass.

We came upon a crowd of men all furious at the poor woman, who stood there, with the bowl of "sasswood" in her hand, calling on God to witness the scene and hear her statements. She stood talking to the "sasswood" for several minutes. A young man stood by her side holding a handful of little stones. As she mentioned each deed that she had been accused of, and declared that she was innocent of it, he would take a stone and touch the side of the bowl of poison with it, and then throw the stone away. After making her speech she drank the "sasswood." There was a perfect babel of voices, for the people were excited and all talked at once.

They then brought the woman to town, and we all came back. The "Quee," a secret society in the town, had the case in charge. The women were all in their houses with the doors shut. The men told us to go inside also, for they did not wish us to see what they were doing.

But we stayed outside, and as we were strangers they did not know what to do with us. The Quee desired to parade about the town and did not wish us to see the devil, for the Quee is a devil-society. It is the devil's coming to town that makes the women hide within their houses.

The man who takes the part of the devil has a strange-sounding whistle that he blows; and this, they say, is the devil talking. That we might not see this man they covered him with a blanket, and carried him around upon their shoulders. They passed quite close to us; but there were so many men that all we could see was the blanket.

After we had been in town a short time we learned, that the very man we were expecting to engage for our guide was impersonating the devil. So we knew there was no hope of getting away till the performance was all over. After they had been around the town several times they went out into the bush and took this devil-man down from their shoulders. He reentered by a different road. Coming up to us as if he were quite innocent of all that had been going on, he said that he was ready to go with us. Then we started on our way again.

We went in canoes several miles up the river, until we came to rapids and could go no farther by water. We left the canoes at a town that was near the bank of the river. The king and chiefs received us kindly. They were much pleased to see so many white people— there were seven in our company—and gave us a guide to show us the road to the falls. We walked in the hot sun through the thick jungle and over the hills through the rice farms.

Soon we heard the rush of the waters and knew that we were near the falls. When we reached the place we sat down to rest, for we were very tired. These falls are not, of course, to be compared with some of the world's noted falls in volume of water, nor does the water plunge straight down as at Niagara. Nevertheless, the whole river bed is of rock, and very rough, and the water rushing and foaming over the rocks is a beautiful sight.

We spent several hours there and then returned to town. While we had been absent the king had cooked us a dinner, which he served in two wash basins—the rice in one, and the palm butter in another. We poured the palm butter over the rice and mixed it in with a spoon. Then we all sat around the bowl and had a hearty meal, two of us eating with a single spoon.

We then started down the river on our way back to Tataka. Here we spent Sunday. We had a Quarterly Meeting, at which missionaries and children were present from nine stations. Eleven were baptized. After dinner we went into the town and held a meeting, and two more were baptized.

On Monday morning we started down the river on our way to Cape Palmas. We reached Bolobo, the end of our journey on the river, at three o'clock, and from there started on through the bush. We came to the native town Quitiqui just before sundown and decided that we had better stay there all night.

Miss McNeil and I, the only ladies in the party, had a small house to ourselves, and the gentlemen another. We did not rest very comfortably, since we had no bed, but were again compelled to sleep on the mud floor, with only a blanket to relieve its hardness. We rose early and went as far as Barraky, where we stopped for breakfast, and reached the Cape at four o'clock in the afternoon.

The night we stopped at Quitiqui we heard that two of our young women had run away to a tribe with which our people were then at war. Their husbands were two of the young men who had gone with me up the river. They had left their wives at home with no thought that they would prove untrue to them, for they had both been married according to the rites of the church only a few months before. We were therefore anxious to get home to Garraway to see if the news was true.

It was eight o'clock in the evening of the second day after our arrival at Cape Palmas when we finally got into the boat and pulled out of the river. But the tide being out, the water was too low to allow our boat to pass over the bar. So the boatmen anchored and waited a time, then came back to the landing and said they would start in the night. At midnight they called us. We had gone to the mission house, a considerable walk away, but went down to the boat, only to find that the captain had again changed his mind and now said that he would not leave until daylight. We returned to the mission and lay down to rest for a few hours.

At break of day they called us again, and we started out. The boat was rowed over the bar; but there we again cast anchor, to wait for the wind. The sea was perfectly calm. So we sat in the burning sun, without our breakfasts, until eleven o'clock, when the breeze sprung up. They hoisted the sail, and we started for home. We reached Garraway at five in the afternoon, much fatigued, but very glad to get back again.

The next day we went to the tribe where our two women had fled, to inquire about them and bring them home if possible. The people refused to let them come home, and accused the Garraways of having some of their women. We finally applied to the Liberian government, which sent a commissioner to bring home the runaway wives. The young men and I went with him to get the women; but the people still refused to let them come.

We never have frost in Liberia; but we do have a rainy season, when everything is wet and all the little hollows in the road are full of water. It was a rainy day on which we went out for the women. The long grass hung over the paths. We took the hammock with us; but I started to walk and got wet, and was then afraid to be carried in the hammock. I therefore walked all the way, with the exception of one place where I had to be carried over a very wet stretch of road.

The tribe to which our women had fled was the Nemia people, with whom the Garraways had been at war soon after I reached Africa. The old scores had never been satisfactorily settled; and they kept the women because of the former grievances.

I believe there is no one thing among the people that causes more disturbance than this habit of the women of running away from tribe to tribe. It is a common occurrence among them, and there are few women who have not at some time in their lives run away from their husbands and homes, to be the wives of other men in some hostile tribe.

These two women had no idea of running away when we left on our up-river tour. But a man of the Nemias had come along and induced them to go off with him. African wives hold everything very loosely, and are easily persuaded to change houses and husbands. So these women packed up all their belongings, shut their house doors, and went away, giving very little thought as to where they were going or what they were leaving.

If the Liberian government had been stronger it could have compelled the Nemias to return the women; but when they refused that was the end of it. One of the women is there to-day. The other, after an absence of seven months, was sorry for her folly, and sent word to her husband that she wished to come back if he would only forgive her. She then ran away from the Nemia people and came back to her husband, with whom she has now been living in her own house for several years.

CHAPTER XI.

UPS AND DOWNS.

A New Helper.—A Clandestine Repast.—Burning of the Boys' House.—The Mission House Rebuilt.—Stair Building.—Redeeming Native Girls.—A Midnight Runaway.—Peter.—Summoned to Court.—The Law's Delay.

IN December, 1891, Miss Carlson, a young woman from Brooklyn, was sent to assist me at Garraway. She enjoyed the work and was of great assistance, staying longer than any other of my helpers, being with me six months, when she married one of our missionaries.

In March, 1892, Miss Whitfield, who was going home to America for a rest, wrote asking me to come down to Cape Palmas, where she was, and take three of her school children to keep in our school until her return. I went to the Cape, leaving our own children in Miss Carlson's care.

I had been absent three days when word came that there had been a fire at the Garraway mission and that the boys' house was burned. We had had a house built to accommodate the boys and for our interpreter, who was also in charge of the farm.

But this man's wife had become dissatisfied, and had threatened to leave him if he did not move off the mission ground and build a house for her. As there was no other way to satisfy her, he built a house in the Christian town, and they moved into it. Even then she was not satisfied with his working on the farm, and to please her he also gave this up.

The boys were thus left in their house alone, with one old man whom we had in the mission. I had charged them strictly that they should obey Miss Carlson in my absence, and not go off the farm without her consent. But the first night I was away, after prayers, the boys went to their own house to go to bed, and Miss Carlson, with the girls, retired to rest in the mission house.

The boys' house had a mud floor, and was not fit for them to sleep in without a fire, so in the center of the room a fire was started in the evening. On this occasion they had brought a few vegetables home from the farm, and some of them said, "Let us cook the potatoes, and eat them before we go to bed." They kindled the fire. As they had no pot, they thought a tin can would do, and, taking a firebrand, went to search for one.

After our interpreter had moved out of the boys' house we had made a storeroom of one apartment, and had put up a few planks overhead, thus making a loft. The old mission house was not safe, the frame being of soft wood and badly rotted, as well as eaten by insects.

We used this storeroom to keep things we were not actually using. Only three weeks before we had received our supplies for the year. Every year a quantity of flour, tinned meats, and groceries was sent out to us, since we could not live entirely on the native food. We might have bought supplies with money from the German traders on the coast; but, having no salary, we could not do that. Moreover these things could be sent to us more cheaply from America, where a fund is maintained for the purpose.

These supplies were in the storeroom, and the tinware was in the loft above it. One of the boys climbed to the loft with the firebrand in his hand, and secured a tin can. They had put the potatoes in the tin and had set it on the fire to boil, when they discovered fire in the loft over the storeroom.

They got water and, as they thought, put it out; but as they did not take everything down, there was doubtless some fire still left. The potatoes were cooked and eaten, and then the old man said he was going to fish in the morning and wanted the boys to go with him to find crabs for bait. All the boys went along except two, who lay down to sleep.

The crabbing party had been away some time and were coming home, when they saw the end of the house in a blaze. Rushing up the hill, they found the two boys still fast asleep. They woke them up and got them out. But there was not time to save their clothes or books. My organ was there, too, for we used this house for school and religious services on account of the insecurity of the mission building.

The boys got the organ outside; but it was badly damaged and was never of any use after this. The house was burned to the ground, with all the supplies for the year, many useful tools, our gun, and other things that we have not yet been able to replace.

It was a black-looking home to come back to, for not only the boys' house was burned, but the fowl house and eleven fowls with it. The cook house also, and the trees and bushes were black all around.

I had labored very hard to get our work up to where it was, and we had all felt that our house was quite homelike. But this fire broke it all up, and we were left without a house that was safe to live in. Several times during thunderstorms, when the wind did seem as if it would blow the house down, we have all gone outside into the rain, knowing that the house was liable to fall at any moment.

One Sunday afternoon the iron side plating of the building began to come off during a windstorm. Some of the large boys got up on chairs and held it with their hands until we could all get outside. Then they leaned a heavy stick of timber up against it until the wind was over and they could nail it up again. That day our house was almost blown down. More than once I have got up in the night and prepared for the worst, thinking that if it did fall I should at any rate be upon my feet. This experience shook my nerves, and was not easy to get over.

We built a small native house in which to have school and services, and had to move into it while the leaf thatching was still green and the mud floor wet. We set up our bed upon boxes and built a fire under it in the afternoons, that we might not take cold from the wet floor. During the day we dried the floor by making fires upon it. Here we lived for three months and a half while the mission house was taken down and rebuilt.

Mr. Robertson, the missionary from Grand Sess, twenty miles above us, came in one evening on his way home to his station, and offered to come and help us rebuild the mission house if some one would carry on his work while he was away; so Miss Carlson went to his station to stay while he came to help us. But he had only got the frame up and began to put on the siding when he got word that Miss Carlson was very sick. They were engaged to be married, and Mr. Robertson went home and married her while she was yet sick, and then took care of her until she recovered.

We were thus left without anyone to help us with our house, except our native young men and boys. But we worked away, however, doing one thing at a time and not knowing until we got to it how we should do the next.

Our presiding elder came to visit us, and remarked as he looked round the house:

"Yes, Miss McAllister, but it takes a carpenter to put up the stairs."

"Yes, I know that," I replied; "but we have not come to the stairs yet. When we do come to them there will be some way for us to get through. You know we are not very particular—we do not want winding stairs."

We worked away, and it was wonderful how the good Lord helped us. We set up the rafters, put on the roof, and fitted the doors and windows.

Ups and Downs.

When we came to the stairs we first found two strong boards long enough to reach to the top landing and touch the ground. We knew we must place them slanting in order to get up and down. Two boards from the old floor answered the purpose. These we set up and nailed in position. We had used up our supply of new nails. And now we had to use the burned ones, raked out of the ashes, and the holes had to be drilled with a gimlet.

For steps we first cut a board long enough to fit between the two slanting planks, and guessing about how far we could comfortably step up, nailed cleats and put in the steps. We then stepped up on it to see how it answered. It seemed to be all right. So we sawed a piece for the rise and fitted it in.

Then we put up another step and tried it, and then a third. We came to the conclusion that our plan was all right. We accordingly made the remaining steps the same way, and felt that we had finished the hardest part of the house. We moved in before the partitions were up, in order to escape from the smoke in the native hut.

This was the hardest year of my work in Africa. Along with all this extra work and that caused by our larger family, I was alone after Miss Carlson went away, and at the same time had eczema in my left hand so badly that part of the time I was not able to dress myself.

But the Lord was good and sent me relief. My only sister came out in April, 1893. No person who has not been in such circumstances can know how I appreciated a sister in my time of need. Truly our kind heavenly Father spared me from burdens greater than I could have borne alone.

Girls are articles of trade in Africa. Consequently they are not free to come to school until they are redeemed. The price of a girl varies in different tribes; but a fair value is two bullocks, one cow, one goat, one brass kettle, six fathoms of cloth, one red cap, six wash basins, one dozen of china plates, a few brass rods for making bracelets, several bead necklaces, and some finger rings and earrings. While negotiating for a wife a man is at the call of his intended mother-in-law to go whenever or wherever she chooses to send him.

But when we redeem the girls to take them into our school we pay the family the money they would receive from a man if he took her for his wife, and are free from any further obligation. These girls are educated, and are not allowed to be sold again, but become the wives of our Christian men and boys.

I had paid the usual price for our oldest girl. Had she remained with her people she would soon have been married, for she was thirteen, and all the native girls aspire to have a husband by that time, and are looked down upon as not being very desirable if they do not obtain one. Our girl was the first redeemed in our tribe; and I often heard the people ask her when we went to town, "Have you not got a husband yet?" or, "Are you not going to get married?"

We hoped to keep her in school until she should learn enough to become a useful woman in our work, and then to have her marry one of our schoolboys and be a help in the native work.

But a young man in town, who had no wife, on hearing that she was redeemed thought it a good chance to get a wife without having to pay for her. So he induced her to leave the mission; and one night she ran away, taking with her the second girl, a year younger than herself.

It was on a Saturday evening. We had all been to town to hold service, and after coming home were preparing to retire, when one of the little girls, who had a sore foot, complained that it was hurting her, and I sent the two older girls to wash it before they went up stairs. I went to my own room and prepared to retire. The girls took the lamp up stairs with them—a thing I had not allowed them to do alone. They soon brought it down and went back to bed.

After I was asleep the two girls came to my door and said " Good-bye " without waking me, and went away in the dark night. They went to the waterside town where the young man was engaged in trading. The other girls knew they had gone, but said nothing until morning.

When I learned that the girls were gone I sent at once to the man I had paid the money to, for he was the older girl's father, and had promised to help me care for her. But he had gone to his farm, and so did not come. We did not know what had induced the girls to leave, and did not know where to find them. They were both from the interior, and I did not know where they could go, unless back home.

We proceeded with the services of the day, which was Sunday. In the afternoon we went to town, as was our custom. When we came to the waterside village the people told us that the girls had arrived there in the night, and that the young man I have mentioned had announced that he was going to marry our oldest girl. The two would have been already on their way to the Cape to be married if there had been any boat to carry them.

But there being no boat, he had taken the girls along the road to their home in the interior. Our Christian men and boys were with me; and they said, "If we get hold of Peter we will teach him sense." He was one of their own tribe, and so were the girls. The native people never think of applying to the Liberian government in cases of this kind. They have their own laws, and settle their own difficulties.

It was getting late, and we started home to the mission. On our way whom should we meet but Peter! He was alone; and we stopped and asked him about the girls. He answered, that he knew nothing about them. I replied: "You need not say that, for we know better. We are just from the waterside, where the people have told us what you have done and what you want to do."

I questioned him, but he refused to answer. So I said: "I am too tired to stand here to wait for you to talk. Come with us to the mission house, I want to ask you some questions." We all went to the mission house and sat down. But Peter refused to talk for a time, until one of the men said, "If you do not talk we will tie you up, and you will not get out of here to-night."

With that he told us where the girls were, and that he intended to marry the older girl. We declared that he should not have the girl, and that to make sure of the return of both the girls we should keep him until they were brought back. We had learned a lesson when the two women of our tribe had run away some time before.

The young men got a rope and securely tied him. We kept him so all night, and I sat up and watched him. In the morning one of the young men went to town and came back with a pair of handcuffs and with irons for the feet and, removing the rope, put these on.

The older girl's father came at last. He was very angry, and said that he would take charge of Peter, and that no one should loose him until he gave his consent. The man for whom Peter had been working also came to see about him. I told this man that it was a native palaver (dispute), that the native people had it in hand, and that it was not I who was holding Peter. "Well, if that is the way," replied the man, "I have nothing to say."

Another young Liberian came and said a great many hard things. But when he saw that I was not afraid and could give good reasons for all that was going on he quieted down; and after eating some molasses—for we were making molasses from sugar cane—he went away quite appeased.

The girls came back in the afternoon, and a crowd gathered. After some loud talking and all but a fight, the older girl's father, who had Peter in charge, let him loose, telling him he must pay him for his trouble.

Five days after this the sheriff was sent, by the Liberian government, to arrest me. The summons stated that I should appear in the court then about to meet. I was to go back by boat with the sheriff.

Leaving the children in charge, I went with the sheriff. Nothing was proved. The case was therefore laid over until the next meeting of the court, three months later, and I was put under bonds.

I had appeared at court, with three witnesses. After being detained for seventeen days, our presiding elder wrote to the judge asking why it was that I was kept so long without anything being done. The judge wrote back that I could go home if I liked. I took the first boat home, for my work was suffering, as there was no competent person in charge. I found all well and everything in order. But it was a real Paul and Silas case!

The foreman or "captain" of the jury was a Christian man who could sympathize with me in my work among the people. He said that he had learned by trying experience that the government did not always help the Christians. He advised me if I had any trouble of the kind again to just move it off the mission grounds, and then no one would say anything.

These were trying days. How often it is that a missionary is called upon to bear one burden after another, until it does not seem possible to endure another! But always when we reach this point relief comes in some unexpected way. This has been my experience; and to-day I praise God for all the past and trust him for the future.

CHAPTER XII.

SASSWOOD PALAVER.

Death of the Two Brothers.—The "Quee."—A Woman Endures the Test.—Witch-hunting Women.—Palaver.—"We Will Give Everybody Sasswood."—"Let's Give Them Some Water."—The "White Plate" of Peace.

WHEN the Cape Palmas and Rock Town people were at war a young man from Garraway went to look on, and, standing too near, was shot in the leg. After a few weeks he died. His brother, who came home to see him, got there just a few hours after he was buried. He, in turn, had not been home more than ten days when he was taken sick and soon died. For two brothers, strong young men, to be taken within a few weeks in this way was an occasion of superstition among the people. They all believed that some witch had been the cause of their death, although they say when a person dies that "God took him."

The morning after the last young man died we went to town. They had made up a bed with boxes, spread his mat on them, and laid him out there. The body was washed and the face streaked with paint. A large new cloth had been put over him; beads were strung about his neck; a pipe lay on his chest, with the stem toward his mouth, and a comb by his head. They had built a canopy over him for shade, and for decorating used cloth of all kinds and colors, hats, caps, coats, and umbrellas. Tables and stands were set around the house, with looking-glasses, pictures, and all kinds of fancy and common dishes on them—a regular variety store, as it looked.

As we approached the town we heard the call of the "Quee"—a secret society of men, called by some "the Devil Society," though the native name is "Quee." We knew when we heard them that they would not bury the man without palaver, and most likely would accuse some one and compel him or her to drink the sasswood. We went at once to the headman of the Quee, and I begged him not to give sasswood. He was in a great hurry, and did not want to be talked to; but I caught his arm and held him with both my hands. I knew him well. At last he said he would not allow sasswood to be given. I asked him if he meant it, and he said he did.

Several men came to persuade me not to have anything to do with the case, and wished to shut me up in a house. But I said, "Don't anybody dare put his hands on me." I knew that if they once took hold of me they would soon put me into a house; for it was against their custom for a woman to see or be seen while the Quee was out, and I was the only woman now outdoors, all the native women being shut up in their houses and not daring to open the door till they received permission from the society. If a woman sees the Quee she has to pay a heavy fine, and all the women and girls are afraid to go out while the Quee is at work, for they are taught, and believe, that it is really the devil that has come to town. It is only the warriors, of course, dancing, singing, and beating drums and cymbals; and the devil is a man blowing a whistle with a peculiar note.

I started back to where the corpse was. On my way I came to where the chiefs were talking, and I sat down with them and listened. They spoke very encouragingly for a few minutes, as if they had determined not to resort to the sasswood, then turned to me and said:

" Teacher, do you hear what we say?"

" Yes," I answered, " and if you do as you say here and not give any sasswood I shall be very glad."

They all rose up to go to where the corpse was, but did not know what to do with me, for the Quee had now passed through the town and gone to ask the dead body who had killed him. I saw they were confused and said:

"Come on, I am going, too."

"O no," they replied. "Woman no fit to go there to-day. Don't you see all women go inside? You must go inside."

"No," I said, "I can't go in any house to-day; I am going to see what you men are doing."

I then led the way. Some said to me, "No, don't go there." But I laughed, and then they laughed. We walked along, I about two steps ahead of them, till we came close to the place. They had run a rope and hung cloth over it, thus inclosing a small yard, and inside this the Quee was at work. As soon as they saw me some called out, "O, there is teacher!" I said, "Yes, and who is this?"

With that I drew the curtain aside and shoved my way through the warriors, who were seated in a circle inside the curtain. They hushed the devil and got him out of the ring. Some scolded, some proposed to carry me into the house, and some laughed. I marched round the circle and said that I had come to bury the man, and that it was time now to carry him to the grave. Some of the men took hold of my arm and said, "Come and sit down, teacher; come inside, the sun is too hot." But I told them that I had not come to sit down, and that I had an umbrella. I told them how foolish it was to have such a performance over a dead man, and that we all must die, and then preached Jesus to them. Meantime, the Queen had removed into a house and were going through their performances there. After giving them enough for a funeral sermon I went into a house for a few minutes for a drink of water, and then came back and sat down with the kings and chiefs.

They told me that it was the devil that was causing the wonderful excitement and making the queer noise.

"No," answered I; "I can tell you who it is."

"Who is it?" they asked, supposing I did not know, because the identity of the man who impersonates the devil is a great secret among them.

"It is Zanier" (Butterfly), I replied; "that is his house," pointing to it.

The kings were much surprised, and said:

"Just look; teacher knows everything! Who has been to tell you?"

"It is not hard to tell who that is," said I. "It is not a secret. It is not you only who do this kind of fashion. The time I went up Cavalla River I saw the people do this, and the man we took as a guide to the Falls was the man who played 'devil.' We sat in town and saw it all. When we would not go into the house they covered him with a blanket, and when they were through they carried him out into the bushes and he soon came round the other side ready to go with us, and we all started up the river."

The kings and chiefs all laughed and thought it a fine joke, but said that I must not tell the women. I did not make any promises.

Soon a young man came to tell me that they had taken a woman to give her sasswood. I went out in the bush where they were. Some of the younger men were there, but none of the headmen who had authority to stop the proceedings. As the younger men would not be persuaded, but said that unless the "big" men sent them word they could not let the woman go, I left them and went into the town to find the headmen. I had been in town only a few minutes when they brought in the woman. She had drank the sasswood—three basinfuls—and carried the wooden basin in her hand. The driver behind her had the pot in which the liquid had been mixed, and he cried out, "A witch! a witch! a witch!"

About three o'clock in the afternoon they buried the man; and the accused woman vomited the sasswood before night. But they would not admit that she was innocent, and took her back to drink more next morning. I did not go. But the Christian men from our " Zion " village and some of the kings went to beg for the woman; and they let her go and did not give her any more sasswood. The Quee concluded to let the matter drop.

After several days had passed the women themselves took up the case. They said that the men did not have " a strong heart " to do anything, so they were going to find the witch. There is no regular society among the women, like the Quee; but they all join together when they wish to accomplish anything, and the men are afraid of them, for they say that the women are stronger witches than the men.

One evening while still in this town we were disturbed after retiring by some person at the door calling the woman of the house. She lay asleep on her mat, with her infant by her. Being awakened, she answered the call and opened the door to see who it was. As she did so I saw several persons there, and heard them call out, " Whee! whee! " She went out, shutting the door after her, and they all went off. This was new to me. I called one of the girls and asked what it meant. At first she did not know; but after listening to the conversation of the people outside she said they were catching people to give them sasswood.

At that moment the family with whom we were staying rushed into the house, threw themselves on the floor, and began to cry. We got up and dressed. I went out to find Scere, whose house we were in and whose wife they had taken. He told me that they had caught five persons. Everybody was quiet, fearing what would come next, and daring to tell me hardly anything.

I induced a young man, a son of one of the women they had caught, who was sitting on the ground crying, to go with me to Zion village. I wished to see our Christian people, who would be able to explain their custom of administering the sasswood. We woke them up, and they said:

"Well, we never saw our people give sasswood at night. If they do it will be a new thing. They will keep the prisoners till morning. The women do not dare to give them sasswood privately, or the people would say they had killed them. There will not be anything done till morning. But it is evident they mean to kill some person."

They told me that in Fish Town, fifteen

miles away, they had killed nine people with sasswood in one day.

We all expected a serious time, and perhaps several deaths. We were very sad; but nothing could be done until morning. So I returned to the town, and found they had caught four more after I left, and that all the nine had been taken to other towns and put under guard till the next day. The women being gone out of the house where we stayed, I did not expect any breakfast there, so asked a neighbor to cook some cassada for me. Then we went back to bed.

We could not sleep and were all up very early. The poor babe had cried for its mother all night. After going through the town to see what was going on and what could be done, I was called to breakfast. The man—Hemie—whom I had asked to cook it for me, had a good meal ready of palm butter, fish, and rice.

Our Christians all gathered together, and we started for the place where the people were assembling to give the sasswood. Upon entering the town where the victims were I went into a house, not knowing that the head women were assembled there to arrange for the palaver. They looked at me, and some said, "What shall we do now? Teacher has come, and we don't want her to know." Another said, " O, she can't understand what we say; let us go on." Another said," Yes, she does; let us go to another town." I said, in their language, for the women cannot understand English, "Yes, I hear what you say, and that is just what I have come for; so you may as well talk away."

Then they all rose up in great confusion and said they would go to the next town, and they all started to run. I said: "All right, I will go there. That is all I have to do to-day—just to follow you around and see what you are doing." Soon they were out of sight. We gathered together and went to the town whither the women had now gone, and where the people were going to give the sasswood. We walked along very slowly, feeling very sad and helpless and expecting to have our hearts made still more sad by the death of one or more of the prisoners, all of whom I knew, and some of whom were my special friends.

When we reached the ground the people were flocking in and seating themselves in companies. The victims were by themselves. The kings and the chiefs who had come to plead for the lives of the accused were in another group; and the relatives of the victims in still another, crying. The women who had the case in hand came from six different towns, and had divided themselves up into many companies, that those who came to plead for the victims might get tired going round to them all, and so give it up.

We went off under the shade of a tree by ourselves, and knelt down to ask God to help us in this time of great need; for we felt that we did not know where to begin or what to say that might have effect. We sat there a few minutes and watched them get ready to beat the sasswood.

One of the kings arose and went to beg the women not to give the sasswood; but they refused to hear and kept up a noise so that his voice could not be heard.

They then brought forth one of the victims —a woman—and poured out some of the sasswood. One of the men got up and talked, but there was no listener. The women began, two by two, to come up to the victim, who had the sasswood before her, ring a bell in her ear, and order her to drink the sasswood.

One of our men said, "I'll interpret anything you say to-day." So I got up and went forward among the rest. We went to one company of the accusers, and they said, "Go to the others." We went to all, and then to the victims, asking them not to drink the sasswood, and assuring them that if they did not do it themselves the people could not make them. But waiting to have everything interpreted was too slow work for that day; so I broke out into the native language, and the ridiculousness of it all came before me, and I began to laugh at it all.

The kings begged, and the Zion men talked to everybody that would listen. I went to the young men who were beating the sasswood, and said: "Let me help you. We will give everybody sasswood to-day. You have not half enough sasswood in the mortar. Let me put in some more. Why, is this all the sasswood you have brought? That won't be half enough. You must send some men to the bush to get more. Don't you see all these people?" The men stood up and laughed, and could not understand me.

I went to the victim, who was sitting over the basin of sasswood, and, after tasting it, said to her: "It is not nice. Don't drink it. It will kill you. We will not get tired of begging for you." Then, going to the women who were ringing the bells, I said: "I am sure you must be tired. Let me ring the bell awhile." The kings were weary from their efforts to save the victims, and declared that they would not permit the women to give the sasswood to two of the prisoners, who belonged to another tribe, and whom they were going to take to town. So they took the two, saying that the women might do what they would with the rest.

We sang and preached Jesus, and told the people of the better way, begging them to choose that day which way was the best. A man in the company sent word to me to be strong and not to let the victims drink the sasswood.

I asked the women if they themselves had drunk sasswood in town that morning. "No," they said. I told them I knew they did not like it, and that it was for the same reason that the victims did not want it. They were amused at the mistakes I made in speaking their language, and some of them, though vexed at me, could not help laughing, and talked quite sensibly to me.

The sun was very hot, and everybody began to get tired; but still the first woman sat with the basin of sasswood untasted before her. They brought another woman and gave her a bowl of it. They began to urge the two women to drink it, as they were getting hungry and wished to go home and cook their meals. So we said: "Go, and bring the pots and rice here and cook it. We are not going to town to-day. We are going to drink sasswood, and you need not be in a hurry. Look, Garraway people have stopped 'cutting farm.' See them all here to-day. They do not intend to have a rice farm this year. If they drink sasswood and kill all the witches they won't be sorry, if they don't see any rice and palm butter."

At this point I was called aside by one of the men, who said that a boat had just come from the Cape bringing our supplies for the year, and word that Brother Nichols, the teacher in the seminary, who had been very ill and had left a few weeks ago to go to the island for his health, had died on board the ship and been buried at sea near Sierra Leone; also, that Brother Garwood, on the Cavalla River, had been drowned. I stopped for a minute, then said to the man: "God has taken them, and her will soon be here for me. Let me do what I can while I live. They are gone now."

I went into the midst of the people and told them what I had heard, saying, "Nobody will think of drinking sasswood for them. All kinds of people die, and we who are here will soon die too." Then I said: "This sasswood is hot. These people cannot drink it. Let us give them some water." Everybody was becoming quiet. So I poured out the sasswood, washed out the bowl, put some water in it, and said, "Perhaps they will drink that."

A man in the crowd, fearing that I might get the prisoners to drink the water, sent me word not to let them. I went back and said: "This water is not fresh. It has been here all day. Let us pour it out, and go to town and get fresh water." I emptied the water out of the bowl and pot, and put the bowl on top of the pot and the pestle on top of the mortar—the people looking on, glad, I presume, to see an end of it all.

I said: "Somebody can carry these things. Come to town. We are all hungry." I took the victims by the hand, raised them up, and we all started for the town. On the way we met some of the older women, and they were angry and scolded; but we all crowded on into town. Some of the people thanked us as we walked along, some laughed, and others scolded. We passed on to the second town, the men taking several of the victims to Zion. The rest, lost in the crowd, found their way to their own houses.

I went to Scere's house to wash my face, which was spotted red and white from the scorching sun. My feet were blistered. After a wash, and after becoming somewhat cooled off and having something to eat, I went to the mission to see about the goods which had come by boat. I had to pay off the carriers who had been helping the boys; but the boys had done very well, and had all the things stowed away.

Toward evening we all went to take the accused women who were in Zion to town. We took them to the headman's house, and he called the rest of the principal men. We told them that these were the women who had been taken to drink sasswood in the morning, and that we had rescued them, and now brought them to their own houses. They thanked us, saying that we had done well, and that they were glad we had done so, and that we must do so always. We then took the women to their own houses.

I had narrowly escaped a sunstroke. Even yet, when the sun is hot I have a severe headache from this day's exposure.

The next day was Sunday. I had slept in Scere's house; and before I was up the women came in one after another to thank me for what I had helped to do for the people, shaking my hand and pulling my arm as expressions of their gratitude. I do not think that since I went to Africa I have shaken hands with more people at one time than I did that morning. I then took the children and went home to have a quiet day.

In the afternoon Scere came up to see me. He told me that after we had come home the head women of all the towns went to the king's house, taking with them a china plate. They begged his pardon for what they had done, and assured him that, since they were convinced that the king's family, to which all the victims belonged, had joined the mission, they would never again take them for sasswood. Finally they had given the king the white plate as a sign of peace between them and as a pledge of their word.

CHAPTER XIII.

THE AFRICAN WOMAN.

Naming a Child.—Peculiar Treatment of Young Children.—Native Jewelry.—Learning to Work.—Marriage Customs.—Domestic Duties.—Outdoor Work.—Harvest Feasts.—Building Houses.—Fishing.—Women in Public Life.

WHEN a child is born in Liberia some member of the family is sent at once to the devil-doctor to inquire who it is and what its name shall be.

The devil-doctor's deeds are all done in the dark. He goes up into the housetop, which is a small windowless attic used as a storeroom and rice granary. He takes with him the cowhorn. This he blows to call the devil; and the devil is supposed to tell who it is that has come back to this world. For the people believe that every newborn child is some deceased member of the family who has returned to life among them. It sometimes receives the same name it had before, and sometimes the name is changed.

When the devil-doctor has blown his horn long enough to call the devil and receive an answer he begins to tell whose child it is by describing the parents. Sometimes he has already heard of the birth and knows the family; but it sometimes happens that he has had to guess, in which case he often makes serious mistakes. The people do not always believe in him; but it is their custom to consult him, and it is hard to break it up.

After finding out who the parents are, and whether the child is a boy or a girl, the devil-doctor goes on to describe it. The inquirer must come prepared to pay for the information with plates, cloth, and tobacco. The devil-doctor may say, for example, that the child is (or was) the mother of a certain man named Scere. In that case she will be called *Scere-day*, or Scere's mother, *day* meaning "mother." If the child is a boy it will, perhaps, be declared to be some great man who has died; and if so the babe will be much respected.

When a son was born to Kalenky—one of our chief men—the father sent to the devil-doctor to inquire who it was that had returned to the earth. The doctor said it was a great warrior named Wear, and that they must train him for war, as he had come to protect them.

When this was told to the father he brought a gun, a powder case, a shot bag, a war dress, and a fringe for the waist made from palm leaf, charms for the head, neck, arms, waist, knees, and ankles, and another peculiar charm in the shape of a cake of soap. This last, moistened with a little water, was to be rubbed with the hands on the infant's skin. They say it toughens the skin so that no shot can pierce it; and a soldier that has this charm need not fear the enemy. All these things were brought and laid on a mat by the side of an infant but a few hours old.

I have sometimes seen infants without anything on their bodies, not even the string of beads which they think so necessary. A child usually wears one of these about its neck, several around its waist, and others on its wrists and ankles. When it is a few days old its ears are pierced, and small rings are put in, or, if the rings cannot be had, a piece of fine wire or a cotton thread.

The child is washed three and four times a day in hot water, and rubbed with a white mixture like paint. Every morning when it is washed several of the older women are called in. Some of them are very competent, and they take charge of the babe. A young mother is never left with the care of her child. These nurses may be seen any morning sitting on one of their common "chairs," which is no more than a stick of stove wood—

outdoors if it is warm, otherwise in the house—with a pepper board by their side. They will rub one of their fingers in the pepper on the board, then thrust it as far down the child's throat as possible, and rub and stretch the throat thoroughly until the poor child is almost strangled and throws up all that is in its stomach. This looks like unmerciful treatment; but they believe it necessary to the child's health and strength. The child is then given an injection of some herb, and laid down to sleep on its little mat on the floor by the fire. Many infants die very young, and I fear that this severe treatment is sometimes to blame.

When the child gets to be nine or ten months old small bells are tied to its person, at its wrists, waist, and ankles. These are intended to coax it to walk. When it moves the bells will tinkle. Pleased by the sound, it will be induced to make another movement, and so will learn to go alone. The mother at this time will take her child to the devil-doctor, and he will make a charm for it which will be tied around the waist.

When the child begins to walk they put on its ankles the native "gless"—a kind of anklet made with several small bells in each ring. From six to ten of these are put on each ankle. No child is supposed to learn to walk without these assistants.

But to return to the children one sometimes sees not dressed in the usual way. I have inquired the reason of the mother when I have seen one of these babies looking so uncared for. I have been told that the child is supposed to be some one who has come from the spirit world only to find articles to carry back, and that if they should dress it or give it anything it would not stay, but would take the things and be gone. Therefore they do not give it anything to wear; and so, since it has nothing to take with it, it is obliged to stay here and grow up. They hope that thus it will change its mind and consent to live with its people.

When a girl is from six to ten years of age she wears on her forearm brass rods, sometimes simply twisted in a spiral, and sometimes bent into separate rings. These are put on halfway up to the elbow—put on with a hammer to stay. They are worn night and day until the flesh becomes sore. Then they may be taken off, for the scars will always be there to prove that she wore jewelry when she was young.

If a woman grows up without these marks on her arms it is a lasting source of annoy-

Children in an African Rice Field.

ance to her; for if her neighbors become vexed with her and wish to insult her, they cast it up to her that her mother was a poor woman and could not afford to put jewelry upon her children. This is a great reproach to a woman, as they all aspire to be reputed wealthy.

The little girls, as soon as they are able to follow their mothers to the farm and the bush, go along to help them; and when they are quite small, not able even to walk all the way, the little daughters may be seen coming home from the farm with their mothers. After having carried one on her back most of the way, the mother will put her down to walk and give her a stick of wood to carry on her head, although she is too small to carry a wood rack, or "banna."

The mother always keeps on hand a small waterpot for her little daughter to learn to carry; and the child may often be seen coming along the road before or behind her mother, with the water splashing over her from the pot, in her first attempts to imitate her mother.

The father will make a little wood rack for her, and she will have a small fanner for fanning rice. Her highest ambitions are to beat her mother's rice, carry a big load of wood on her head, and have her own farm. Then she is considered by all to be a smart girl and fitted to make a smart wife for some man.

A girl is often betrothed at the age of seven, and sometimes while she is yet an infant in her mother's arms. She is sold to be the wife of whatever man may choose to purchase her.

At about the age of ten or twelve years she is taken to live with her betrothed's people, where she will be associated with him and learn "his fashion." She is supposed to study his wishes and live to please him. Some of the men make slaves of their wives, and do not consider that any of their wishes are to be consulted; while others are not so, but treat their wives with a great deal of respect and try to please them, so that they live very happily together.

The girls in Africa reach mature womanhood much earlier than in America. At the age of fourteen or fifteen they are married. The marriage ceremony is very simple. When a man takes his betrothed to be his wife he has a fowl killed and some rice cooked. They both partake of these, and it is understood by all that the pair are henceforth man and wife. They really have no marriage ceremony at all.

A man generally has one favorite wife, or head wife. A man may choose his own wife; but his family—which is the whole family connection—pays for her. Upon his death his women, who are family property, are divided up among the other members. The head wife has charge of all the rest, unless they refuse to submit to her, in which case they live entirely independent of her, while doing their part toward caring for the husband.

A man has from three to twelve wives, according to his wealth and importance. If a man has the reputation of being a good husband, he often gets wives without paying for them. They run away from other tribes and come to him, hoping to better their condition. But if their lot turns out to be no better than with their former husbands they often go back to them again.

A man in going off to his work in the morning is never sure that he will find his wife at home when he returns in the evening. It is a common thing for wives to run away; and she is considered a queer woman who at some time has not run away from her husband or for some reason been separated from him.

In going visiting a man generally takes one of his wives with him to carry his chair, light his pipe, get his bath water ready for him, run errands, and wait upon him generally.

Some of the women are very good housekeepers, and have a place for everything and keep everything in its place; while others, like some of our civilized women, never seem to have a place for anything and keep a very untidy house.

A good housewife in Africa will always rise before it is light enough to see well. To be sure, they have no clocks; but as the fowls sleep in the house, on a perch behind the fire, the roosters are as good as an alarm clock, for they never fail to crow at three o'clock, and again at the break of day. It is thus an easy matter to wake up at about the same time every morning—much easier than to sleep, for the hens will descend from their perch and wander about, walking over the sleepers stretched on the floor, unless some one rises and opens the door to let them out.

I know this to be a fact, for I have often slept in the native houses. One night five of us slept in a circular house fifteen feet in diameter, with twenty-one fowls on the perch, a fire burning, and the doors shut tight, so as not to allow any witch to enter. It really felt as if there were some witch inside, and I fear there was more there to harm us than there could have been outside.

The first thing in the morning after letting the chickens out is to light the fire, which has generally died out, or almost out, during the

Woman's Work in Africa.

night. The next is to fill the large pot with bath water from the waterpot. While the bath water is being heated the woman refills her waterpots. Generally by the time she has this done the others are up, and she can sweep her floor. When the bath water is hot she has her bath, taking with her, it may be, her child of three years, who is washed with the same towel and water. She combs her own hair, as well as that of the child; then, putting a little native perfume on her hands, rubs some on her own face and body. The child is treated in the same way. She is then ready for the day's work.

The remnant of the evening meal is warmed up for breakfast, often a little cassada or some other vegetable being cooked to eat with it. After breakfast is eaten, if it is not the rice-planting or cutting season, the housewife takes her "banna" (wood rack) on her head, and her ax and cutlass, and with her baby on her back, goes to her vegetable farm. She weeds out some of the grass, then takes up some vegetables to carry home with her, planting new ones in their place. Then gathering a rack-full of wood she returns to the village.

Perhaps, in the meantime, one of the other wives has given the husband his morning bath, and now it is her turn to give him water for his evening bath. In warm weather he may prefer cold water; but if it is at all cool he wants his bath hot—and the natives can bathe in very hot water.

She then has her rice to beat. It has been placed in the morning in the rack over the fire to dry. She now takes it down, carefully picking up every kernel that may drop, and puts it into her mortar and, with a heavy stick about seven feet long and as large around as she can well hold in her hand, beats it till she can see the chaff coming off. She then puts it into her fanner and fans it in the wind till the loose chaff is blown away. This process of beating and fanning is repeated until all the rice is cleaned. Then she sits down and picks out all the chaff that cannot be fanned out, and the rice is ready for cooking.

In preparing a meal the rice is cooked first, and taken off the fire to simmer over some coals that are drawn out on the floor. Next, the palm butter is made and set aside to cool, for no good cook will serve food that is hot enough to burn one. Finally the vegetables are cooked. These are better eaten hot, and therefore are cooked last. This is all done over a single fire as a rule; but in some cases, when the meal is wanted in a hurry, two fires are lighted, and the dinner is soon ready.

Generally, however, there is no hurry. They do not eat the evening meal—which is dinner—until dark. If it is ready earlier they often wait around until after dark before eating it. This is the big meal of the day. When they eat a hearty meal before retiring, they do without much breakfast in the morning, and sometimes with only a very light lunch, and that not until late in the day.

In "farm-cutting" time they cook a good meal in the morning for the men, for the work is hard. After it has continued for some weeks and the men are getting tired the women prepare the breakfast and take it to the men in the field about eleven o'clock.

This period of "farm-cutting" is the woman's time to obtain a supply of wood. Every day she goes forth, and returns with all the wood she can carry, piling it away neatly in the wood rack to dry for the rainy season. The sticks are about two feet long; and most of their wood is cut from small saplings. With a cutlass, they hack the stick all around, leaving a little bit in the center which is broken off. This leaves one end of the stick of wood all slivered.

These ends are all turned out in the wood rack. When the wood is dry it lights readily, as it is always put into the fire slivered end first. A woman takes great pride in having her house well stowed with wood, and when it is done feels as happy as we do when the bins are filled with the winter's coal.

A very ambitious woman will sometimes take her cutlass and go to help her husband cut farm. But as a rule the women have nothing to do with the farm till it is time for the planting, which is all done by them.

The men build little green booths on the farm, where the pots are often taken to the farm. Sometimes members of the family sleep there, and the victuals are carried out and cooked there. The women take their babies, and everybody turns out to plant rice.

As soon as the rice is up they have to watch the ricebirds, or they will pull it all out of the ground. Then the grass begins to grow, as the ground has not been broken, and it must all be weeded out. The men generally help with this, as well as in keeping the birds from the rice.

When the rice is ripe all hands turn out to cut it, the women being quite as good at this work as the men. While the men may leave the field for other things, the women feel that they must be constantly there until the rice is all out.

When it is cut and brought to town the

women begin to dance; and even before the harvest is finished the evening hours are often spent by the younger people in having a good time. But after the harvest is completed the women especially spend several weeks in dancing and feasting. Great pots of rice are cooked, and everybody enjoys himself.

The women go on dancing parties from town to town, and are entertained by their friends. Often a bullock is killed for the visitors, and they dance all night, and as much of the day as they can stand; and it is the duty of the visitors to show the same honor to the hosts when the visit is returned.

The last months of the year are spent in house building. As the native houses begin to decay in about five years much time is spent in making repairs. It is a good house, and one that has been well cared for, that will last fourteen years. The thatch used for roofing often has to be brought a long distance, and always on the head; for the people have no wagons or carts, not even a wheelbarrow, and no roads except narrow footpaths.

The men go out to the bush, cut the leaves, and start home with them, and their wives meet them on the road and carry the burden the rest of the way. The timbers of the house frame may also need to be carried a long distance, and a good wife is often seen following her husband in the road, with as heavy a load of building poles on her head as he bears on his.

When the house is up and the woodwork pretty well finished the women begin to plaster. The walls are made of narrow pieces of native plank set on end, and need a great deal of plastering on account of the numerous holes. A woman seldom plasters her house alone, but she will invite her neighbor's wife in to help her, and in turn will assist her neighbor when she may be in need. In this way the work is lightened.

The floor is the last thing to be put into a house. The women bring the mud or clay for the floor. The men often help to beat it; but it has to be washed over with a substance which they call "bleen," and this the women always do.

The women can hardly be called fishermen, as the men consider that their work. But there are many shellfish that the women gather, and a very small fish called "necklies," which they catch with a cloth. Four women go together to fish in this way. They wade out into the river until they see a school of these fish. Then they arrange the cloth in the water, two of them holding it, while the other two surround the fish and drive them into the cloth, which is then gathered up like a net, and the fish emptied out into a brass kettle or a bucket brought for the purpose. Then the cloth is let down for another draught. When they are through they divide the fish and return home. These are the smallest fish I ever saw them take for food, being not over three quarters of an inch long.

They also set traps to catch a fish resembling the eel. In time of high water they set these traps in swamps or marshy places. Crabs are often caught along with the fish, and these are generally dried and put away for the dry season, when fish are not so easily taken.

In time of war the women are the messengers, as the warriors—every man is a warrior—are not allowed to go to the enemy's town. A man's life would not be safe; but the women can go in safety, and, as a rule, they are allowed to return. Sometimes they are imprisoned; but if it is known that they have been sent by the other tribe with a message of peace they are generally well received and allowed to return to their homes in peace.

When a woman becomes old and not able to earn more than her own living the husband's attention is generally devoted to his new and younger wives, and his first wife, now being neglected, seeks a better home among her children, generally with one of her sons.

I remember one of these neglected wives, an old woman, who had lived for several years with her daughter. The daughter died, and the old woman's husband, seeing that his first wife's child had died and that she was now homeless, felt it his duty to take her back. He built a little home for her near his own, and supported her in her feeble old age.

When a woman dies all the women turn out to dance, for it is a great honor to the dead to have a good dance at the funeral. Since they all want to be buried with honors they try to be present at every dance, so that when they die themselves everybody will make an effort to be present and dance for them.

When an old person dies the natives never say that some one has witched them, but that their time is finished and God has taken them.

The women exert great influence over the men. In their palavers they do not generally call on the women to say anything unless they have a serious question to settle, when they call upon the women to help them decide.

In case of war, if all the soldiers wished to go and fight, and the women rose up and said, "No, we are not willing, you must not do so," they would all be afraid to go, fearing defeat; for they say, "Woman got witch past man," and they are afraid to displease them for fear of being witched, and so defeated or killed.

Every town has its head woman, and when any person has done what the women think deserves punishment, the men keep silence and do not interfere. I have scarcely found a single man that had courage enough to face the women at such a time and say, "This thing that you are doing is wrong; it shall not be done." I have sometimes asked why it is that the men are afraid to oppose the women, and been told, "Well, woman is the mother of man, and we ought to listen to her."

Some of the women are remarkably good speakers. Not every woman would attempt to rise in a meeting of the people to give her reasons why certain things ought or ought not to be done. But they have certain women who are recognized as public speakers.

The woman in our tribe who was considered the best speaker was called "Queede." I have seen her standing in the midst of a crowd of people seated on the ground—kings, chiefs, soldiers, and women—and talking to them with just as much earnestness and decision, and receiving as much attention, as any man I ever saw.

If the women have anything to say they meet by themselves and then appoint one or more of their best talkers to speak for them in the general council.

Woman is not the downtrodden creature in Liberia that she is in India and many other heathen lands. Yet it is harder to reach the women than the men. They do not seem to have the same desire to rise out of heathenism and receive Jesus. This may be from the fact that they have been more confined to their homes and have not seen so much of the world, and do not realize the benefits of civilization. But some of the women are coming out, and they make good workers when they are saved.

CHAPTER XIV.

FARMING.—AFRICAN CURIOS.

A People of One Occupation.—"Sorrying" a Neighbor.—"Cutting Farm."—Rice Culture.—Vegetable Gardening.—"Casting" a Bracelet.—Articles of Utility and Ornament.

THE natives of Liberia still work their farms according to the rude fashion of their fathers. They have no plows or anything with which to break the ground, except very small hoes. Every year they "cut" or clear a new farm—not always clearing off the heavy timber, but generally that of six or seven years' growth.

They are all farmers, though they all live in the towns. There is, indeed, no other way to make a living. A man may be skilled in some particular line of work—for instance, he may be a competent blacksmith or maker of wickerwork or house builder—without receiving an adequate support therefrom. There is no market or system of exchange among them. A man may do much work for his neighbors; yet his work will bring him little or no return, and if he does not have his own farm he may be very poor.

Thus, he may be a successful fisherman; and yet it would not pay him to spend all his time fishing, for his neighbors, one after another, would come asking him to "sorry" them and give them "just a little bit" for some soup, until he would not have enough left to make "just a little bit" of soup for himself, and so his time would be wasted. If he should refuse to give to his neighbors when they knew he had "plenty fish" he would soon have their ill will and not be able to live among them. Nor would he have any rice unless he made his own farm.

For several miles around the town the land is used for farming; and about once in seven years the same land is cut again, so that when it comes to be used a second time there is quite a growth of timber and vines on it.

In clearing a farm the first thing is to go over it with the cutlass and cut all the grass and vines under the trees and shrubs. After this is done the vines on the trees soon become dry. The farm is then gone over again and all the trees and shrubs cut down; and as soon as the leaves are dry the land is ready for the fire.

On a dry, windy day the farm is set afire. If it is dry it will burn well, and only the larger shrubs and trees will be left. In case it does not burn well, much work is necessary to gather the brush into piles and destroy it.

When all the brush is burned they at once commence to plant. The women plant the rice. With a short-handled hoe about two inches wide they make small holes in the ground, and drop two or three grains of the rice out of a shell which they carry in the left hand. Then with the hoe they cover the rice, and plant another hill about four inches from the first. Thus, the whole farm is planted, the women going around the stumps and over the small logs, and remaining in a stooping position all the time.

The springing plants must be constantly watched from daylight until dark, or the rice-birds will pull them all up. They must be watched until they have taken root so firmly that the birds cannot pull them up. Nor will the birds trouble them again until they head out and begin to fill. Then for about six weeks all hands are again busy scaring off the birds. It is the work of the boys especially to get up before day and go to the rice farm, so as to be there when the birds first appear, their mothers sending their breakfasts out to them. The boys throw stones at the birds with slings.

When the rice is about six inches high vegetables are planted between the rows. When it is about ten inches high the farm is gone over again, and the weeds are pulled that have grown up because the land has not been properly cultivated.

When the rice is fully ripe men, women, and children are kept busy harvesting—at the same time driving the birds away. The rice is cut with a small knife made by the native blacksmiths. This is about the size of a penknife; and when the people see a penknife the first thing they say is, "O how nice this would be to cut rice with!"

Standing erect, they cut one head of grain at a time, and gather them into the left hand until they have a handful. Then they tie this with a rice straw and lay it on the ground. If there are many cutting in the same field one person is appointed to gather up all these handfuls and bind them into bunches.

When the rice is cut it is left to lie in the field for a short time to season. This rice is one thing that is safe from thievery; the people do not steal what is left in this way. It is considered a serious offense for one to steal even a single bunch of it, and if detected the culprit is fined one bullock.

When the rice is taken to the house where it is to be stored the vegetables are left growing on the farm. The women then weed out the grass. When the vegetables are grown they are taken out gradually, enough for a meal at a time, and the farm is allowed to go back to bush again. The next year a new one is cut and worked in the same manner.

In the interior, the natives have a certain time when the women cut a small "farm," as they call it, though it might better be called a garden. Here they plant their pepper, peas, pumpkins, okra, eggplants, and corn. Some of them gather pepper and peas by the bushel, bring them down to the beach, and sell them to the people there, who do not plant them for themselves, as their land is not so good and they are often hindered by war.

Aside from these yearly farms, the people on the beach have a vegetable garden always kept planted. Each woman chooses a small piece of land near the town, where she plants her cassada, their most common vegetable. Every day, when she goes for vegetables for the daily meals, she plants others in their places to ripen for a future day. On this one patch are found vegetables in all stages of growth. Thus she always has a supply of food, in addition to the yearly harvest of rice.

In the interior, where the land is richer and the people are better off, they use fewer vegetables, and eat rice morning, noon, and night.

They say, "Vegetables are hungry chop." But the people who live in the towns on the beach are often glad to get vegetables enough to satisfy their hunger. Besides cassada, there are sweet potatoes, yams, breadfruit, and eddoes. These are all good food, but are not grown in abundance.

What might be accomplished in Liberia if the people cultivated the land and planted every corner as farmers do in America we do not know. But it is certain that they have a rich country, and one where there is a constant growth of vegetation.

The absence of the righteousness that "exalteth a nation" is sorely felt in Africa. The sin that is "a reproach to any people," has blighted that fair land. The people are groaning to-day under the curse of sin; and nothing will better their condition but the blessed Saviour who can remove the curse from their hearts. Then will their lives and their land show that they have a new King—one who delights not in war and blood, but would have them live as brethren, and their land rejoice and blossom as the rose. Lord, hasten the day, and help us to do our part in bringing in the time when light, instead of darkness, and song, instead of sighing, shall fill this fair Liberian land!

African Curios.—I.

In the accompanying illustration the group marked "1" represents ten bracelets, the number usually worn upon one wrist, though I have sometimes seen a larger number. They are of brass and are made by the native blacksmiths. The natives take several kinds of metal out of the ground, and make tools and jewelry.

In making these bracelets they first form a model of beeswax. On a wide board which he has himself hewn from a log with his ax and cutlass, the artist rolls the wax until it is cylindrical in form and of the required size, and adds the desired ornamentation.

He then takes a kind of clay found in the beds of running streams, mixing it to a certain consistency. The wax model is imbedded in the clay, with a small stick inserted in each end. He sets the clay in the sun to dry. When it is thoroughly dried he places it in the fire, leaving it there until the clay is burned hard and the wax melted. Then he takes out the two sticks and lets the melted beeswax run out of the holes in which they were set, and the mold is ready for the brass.

Next, putting his brass in a small earthen pot, he covers it with charcoal which he has made himself by cutting down and burning a hardwood tree. With rude bellows, constructed with wood and goatskins and worked with the hands, he blows the fire until the coals are glowing and the metal in his crucible is melted.

For tongs he takes a palm branch which is elastic enough to answer his purpose, and, lifting the melting pot from the fire, pours the liquid metal into the clay mold. When the mold is full he drops it into water; and when it has cooled he breaks the clay and has a bracelet of cast brass, which is a perfect copy of the beeswax model.

The dancing anklets (numbered " 2 " in the illustration) are made from steel, which is heated in the blacksmith's fire and beaten into shape on his anvil, which is simply a hard rock. They are made with bells, which rattle as the people dance in their bare feet, and make half the music.

The next (numbered " 3 ") represents three bracelets intended for a little girl. They are simply brass rods bent into shape. All the girls begin to wear them at five or six years of age. The arm is covered with them halfway to the elbow, and becomes very sore from the constant friction of the brass. This is really what these bracelets are worn for. I have already explained how proud a woman is of the scars which prove that her mother was rich enough to deck her children with bracelets.

The two articles marked "4" are caps. The one on the left is a genuine native cap; while the other, though of native manufacture, is evidently copied after a European smoking cap. Both are made from the native thread, a fiber obtained from the leaf of the palm tree. The smoking cap has been dyed with herbs and barks.

"Gree-grees" ("5") are charms worn by warriors. These have power—so the medicine man says—to prevent a ball from striking or penetrating the body, to give the warrior great presence of mind in battle, and to make his appearance so hideous that the enemy will lose heart and run away. The small ring at the top is worn on the right arm to make it strong when heavy work is to be done.

The upper pair of the three heavy anklets marked "6" are of solid copper. They weigh eight and a quarter pounds. They are made in molds, like the bracelets, are riveted on, and are worn night and day for years. This pair belonged to the king's wife; and when I went in town to look for some anklets for my collection she brought these out and said:

"When I was in darkness I believed these had a soul; and I thought that when I died I should want to have them buried with me, that I might wear them in the spirit world, as I had worn them here for years. But now I have learned of Jesus, and I don't worship these things. I know they have no soul, and when I go to God's country I won't need them, for I believe God now. So I will let you have them."

The third anklet is of solid iron, and needs to be pried open in order to get it on. The ends are then hammered together. Such anklets are worn for ornament. Not everyone can afford to have them. Those who do wear them are considered fine ladies, although they, like the rest, may have to go to the bush daily for their wood and farm work. Of the two necklaces ("7"), the one on the left is made of seashells and beads, and supports a bell. A child wearing one of these can be heard for some distance. The people admire it, and the children like to hear it. The other is made of small shells called "cowries." These shells are rare, and in some parts of Africa are used for money.

Number 8 represents a common instrument of music called a "zah." It is made from a hollow gourd. The network of cord around the "zah" is decked out with sections of the backbone of a snake. The ends of the cords are held in the left hand, and the handle of the gourd in the right. It is shaken in such a way as to produce different sounds, and all their dancing "tunes" are played upon it. The women play this "zah," while the men beat the drum; and these, with the dancing anklets and the songs of the dancers, make the native music.

Number 9 is a hair comb made from hard wood. Below it is seen a powder case, made from skin, the flasks being cut out of soft wood. This is tied about the waist and worn by the men like a cartridge box. The other article (at the left of the comb in the figure) is a war cap, made from the native palm fiber thread. There is some charm connected with such a cap, which is also worn at times by devil-doctors.

The article labeled "x" is a hand satchel, native made, but not a native idea. The maker of it copied the idea from some lady's hand satchel that he had seen. It is of skin, the edges being nicely embroidered with native rope such as they tie their houses together with. This is split very fine and made smooth with a knife. The ring is put on for ornament; and the little horn is filled with medicine to bring good luck to the owner.

Number 11 is a dagger (and sheath) made from the native steel. This particular dagger has been through many a frightful scene. The case is made of snake skin, and is many years old. I got it from the king; and it had been one of his treasures.

Number 12 is a group of utensils. Above is the large knife, or cutlass, the most useful article a man or woman can have in Africa. With it the native cuts the grass, vines, and bush on his farm, fells the timber and hews the planks for his house. If, as is often the case, he makes his house of bamboo he cuts the poles and splits them with the same tool. If he goes to war he may use it both for sword and dagger.

The African women use the cutlass, along with the ax (shown below it in the figure), to cut wood; and it is her most useful implement. She uses it to weed her farm and to prepare and plant her vegetables. With the cutlass she digs the vegetables for the meal, and it is the knife with which she peels them. If she has flesh meat she divides it with the same blade. The cutlass is, in fact, the handiest article about a house and one that both men and women use in the arts of peace and of war.

In the same group (12) hangs a cow horn, covered with red leather, and used as a powderflask. On the left of this is seen a war bell, such as is worn on each warrior's neck in time of war. It is made of iron, and has an iron ball inside. When the enemy are seen all the

African Curios.—II.

warriors ring these bells and shout at the top of their voices, to terrify them.

Number 13 is a cocoanut just as it grows on the tree. The nut is inside of the large fibrous husk. Hundreds of them may be seen growing on a tree at once, some ripe, some half grown, others just in the bud.

Number 14 is an idol, or fetich, made from herbs and grasses beaten in a mortar and mixed with clay, pot black, and oil. This is spread over a goat's horn and left to dry. A chain, a deer's horn filled with medicine, and two bells are attached to this horn. The idol is wrapped in a monkey skin, leaving the chain and bells hanging out. The whole is tied on a man's back and worn in war as a protection against the enemy's bullets. The man wearing it goes to war with the devil-doctor's assurance that, while he continues to wear it, he is perfectly safe, even in the front of the battle, and that no musket ball can pierce his skin. This is one of their most expensive fetiches, and it is not every man that can afford to have one.

This one has seen service in the wars; but the owner has now accepted Christianity. He sent it, with many others, to the mission, and said he had learned better than to trust in such foolishness and had no more use for it, because he was going to trust in God. He afterward came forward and was baptized.

The bowl which contains this fetich is a common wooden basin. It is used for general household purposes, and is also the one dish in which the family meal is served and out of which they all eat.

The hair hanging from the table is the end of a charm to be carried in the hand when going on a journey. The hair is taken from the tails of slaughtered cattle, and is bound together with a cord such as is used for fishing. On the other end is a piece of iron. A man traveling with one of these in his hand considers himself safe from disease or accident. The women when dancing also carry a similar cow tail, although there is no charm about the one they carry.

The basket on the top of group 15 is a colander woven with the tough stems of a vine called "gah." These stems also form the rope used in binding their houses and for other purposes of cordage. They are split and worked with a knife till smooth and pliable, then woven into this basket form. This is a most handy article, and one without which a woman cannot keep house, since all her palm butter has to be strained through it.

The bowl on the table is made from a gourd,

and is only used for dry articles. The marks on the outside are for ornament and are burned in with a hot iron.

The bag hanging from the table is used by devil-doctors for carrying charms and "greegrees." It is made of deerskin.

The wickerwork on the floor at the right is a wood rack. It is made of vine stems, and is light and strong. The women carry everything in one of these poised on the head, and in many ways it takes the place of a hand satchel. The article inside of the wood rack is a long-haired monkey skin.

On the floor at the left is a king's chair. It is carved out of a solid piece of wood, and belonged to King Charles Hodge. This is no common chair, and it is seldom you meet one like it. The ordinary " chair " on the Kroo coast is a stick of wood. A round block nine inches in diameter and a foot long will make two chairs when split in two, the flat side resting on the floor. Every house has several " chairs " of this sort. Much time is spent in making a chair like the one in the illustration, for it is all carved by hand and with the rudest tools. But there are men who take delight in doing a thing like this, and will spend all their spare moments at it.

A gray monkey skin lies upon the king's

chair; and resting upon one end of the chair and of the wood rack is a "bole-blu"—the seat in which a baby sits and is carried on its mother's back. The white strings are the strips of cloth by which it is fastened to the shoulders.

The cloth on the table is made from native cotton, colored with native dyes, woven in narrow strips, and so sewed together as to give the pattern shown in the figure.

All the native implements, ornaments, etc., described in this chapter were collected by me in Africa, and most of them have been in actual use.

From *Illustrated Africa*.

West African House.

CHAPTER XV.

HOUSE-BUILDING.—THE LIQUOR CURSE.

Preparing the Materials.—The Four Main Pillars.—Ceiling. — Roof and Thatch.— Walls.— Flooring.— " Bleen."— Furniture.—Rum, the Curse of Africa.

THE native house is circular—not by geometry, but by guess. Indeed, sometimes it is noticeably flattened on one side. The African builder has no square and compass with which to test his handiwork; and there is not a straight road or anything else of his construction that would bear a leveling instrument or a straight-edge. He thinks it makes no difference how crooked a line is; and even when there is nothing to hinder him from running a straight fence or road, he finds it easier —and perhaps he would say better—to choose the crooked rather than the straight.

The house-builder has first to fix upon a site. He selects a location in the village, calls the people together, puts down some small "dash," or present, and asks permission to erect his house there. If no objection arises his present is accepted, and he has leave to build.

With cutlass and ax he goes to the bush and cuts timber for the frame. This he carries back to town on his head. If his wives are amiable they may help him; but if not, he has to bear his own burden, unless, as often happens, his near relatives come to his aid.

Having brought in the main timbers he cuts and brings in the trees from which planks are made. The wood of these trees is soft, and they are first cut into lengths and quartered, and then split as small as can well be used, and hewn smooth with the cutlass.

Quantities of a tough, supple vine which grows in the big bush are brought in and piled up, to be manufactured into the rope with which the house is tied together—for not a nail is used in the building.

Next the leaf is procured for the thatch. This is cut and tied in large bundles and transported into town on the heads of men and women.

All the building material, timber, planking, cord, and thatch, is now ready.

Some of the men attain considerable skill as house carpenters. Indeed, few of the natives would be capable of building a house, unaided. A number of houses are generally erected at about the same time, and the people join together and help one another.

After the ground has been leveled off four holes are dug, and four stout posts, each about ten feet long, are planted in them. These inclose a square in the center of the intended house. The ceiling is then constructed. Four large timbers are laid down in the form of a square of the same size as that inclosed by the four uprights. Four other timbers are laid upon these and tied firmly in place. Cross pieces or braces are then tied on, and the square is filled in with split bamboo closely interwoven and well fastened with native rope. The whole fabric is then raised and laid on top of the uprights so as to serve at once as a a ceiling for the main room of the house and flooring for the loft.

Four light poles are cut for the main rafters. These are securely fastened together at one end and placed in position so as to give a conical form to the roof. Other rafters are added until the roof is ready for its " sheeting." For this the rope of supple vine is used. This is wound round and round from peak to eaves and firmly tied at regular distances. It strengthens the roof and forms a foundation to which the thatch is fastened.

The wall posts come next. These are set in the ground at the ends of the rafters, and lengths of the rope are passed around the house at the top to hold them together. Light and flexible hoop poles are passed around the house, about five rounds generally. These are tied to the wall posts, and to these in turn the planking on the inside is tied.

The front door of the house is called the man's door, and the smaller one at the side the woman's door. A few houses have also a third door.

The planks used for sheathing the wall are three or four inches wide, one edge being thinner and more irregular than the other. They stand upright and overlap one another on the side. Any chinks that may be left are carefully filled up with small pieces of wood, and the wall is then ready to be plastered with what the natives call " bleen "—a mixture of cow manure and water.

The leaves for the thatch are large, and when four or five of them are put together they look much like a shingle. They are tied down with the rope. The thatchers begin at the eaves of the roof and work up; and when the top is reached a cap is made for it and securely tied on.

As soon as the roof is completed a fire is built inside the house, and kept burning to smoke and dry the leaf. The house will not last long unless the leaf is thoroughly dried and cured with the smoke. The women on the beach make salt by boiling the sea water in large, flat brass pans; and when a man has put up a new house he often gets two or three of them for a few weeks to boil their salt in it, claiming that the steam from the salt water is good for the roof.

When the roof is thoroughly dry the ground within the house is broken up with a hoe, and a red clay is put in for a floor. This clay is spread five inches deep, and is beaten with a hardwood bat made for the purpose until it is quite smooth and all the lumps are broken. After drying about two days it begins to crack; but nothing is done until it has dried thoroughly and cracked all it will. Then it is gone over again, and all the cracks are beaten together; and they wash it with a preparation which they make from some herb, and which, they think, renders the floor durable and keeps it from cracking. The floor is also washed with "bleen" several times, and left to dry for a few days before being used.

Then the family can move in. A fire is kindled between two of the posts supporting the ceiling. Three rocks, called "glebbies," are prepared for a fireplace and set up together on the floor. They are about a foot high; and the fire is made between them, so as to come up about the pot when it is placed upon them. The glebbies thus serve for a crane.

Over the fireplace is the "boah." This is nothing more than a large box made of poles, bamboo, and rope, and plastered in the same manner as the house. It might, indeed, be called a cupboard, for it is a place to keep rice, fish, meat, and dishes dry and sweet in the smoke. Under this "boah" is a rack on which wood is dried for using. No woman will burn green wood if she can help it. The new rice, also, is dried here, before putting it in the mortar.

Entering the house by the front door, one sees a little pot, bottle, or piece of iron. This contains a charm to prevent anyone from bringing witchcraft or disease into the house. Under the floor is generally another charm to insure the safety of the household. Near this door is the place where one sits down while making a call. The chair is generally there, if there is one in the house; and if not, there is the block of firewood which is the common African seat.

On the opposite side from the fire is the woman's door. Here she does her work. This door is generally obstructed. As the house is small and she has no table, she sits in this doorway to peel her vegetables, prepare her rice for cooking, and wash her bowls and pots —for her husband eats out of a wooden bowl, and she out of the pot if it happens to suit her better.

On the floor at the back of the house stand the waterpots, generally two, and sometimes three. These are filled with water every morning and evening. Hanging on the wall are the bowls and basins, and sometimes the plates. The pots for cooking, if of iron, stand at one side; if of clay, they are put in the "boah" over the fire.

Between the waterpots are the house idols. They are of various sorts, and remain here year after year, with all the dust and dirt of the house gathering upon them. When the man of the house thinks it will please the god, or idol, a fowl is killed in sacrifice to it. The blood is sprinkled on the idol, together with some oil and a white medicine obtained from the medicine man; and the poor, deluded man believes that the wrath of the god is turned away.

It is common to have the limb of a tree, with a number of prongs on it, set into the ground and left standing three or four feet high. On these, as hooks, the drinking cup is hung, and any charms the family may have.

This rack is near the household god, which is supposed to exercise a special power over all charms. A king who possesses a silk hat generally hangs it here when not wearing it.

Back of the fire is a kind of general place for everything, but especially for the hens. A shelf is strung up by means of the ever-useful rope, and on this the fowls roost. A basket or box stands near by, in which a nest is made and the hens are set.

Behind the front door the man of the house hangs his gun, his war "medicine," and the mat on which he sleeps. Over the door is placed a charm to protect the lives of the household. The skulls of all the animals that have been shot by the man are also hung up here as an evidence of his ability to kill game.

Around the outside is made a veranda, about four feet wide, to protect the wall from the rain. A man with little ambition or energy always has an unfinished house; and it is easy to tell, by the look of the hut, what sort of man lives inside. Some houses have under the veranda, by the door, a bench made of bamboo and the inevitable rope. This is generally four feet wide and five feet long, so that they often make a bed upon it and lie down for a rest. In the front door is a hole two inches long and an inch wide. This is intended as a door by which the idol may pass out and in when the man's door is shut!

The floor is kept scrubbed and clean; else the house would not be sweet. It costs no little time and strength for an American woman to keep her floor free from dirt. The African woman, too, feels that her house must be kept clean, and at least twice a week she scrubs her floor. As she has mud and not planks for flooring, she cannot use water; so she goes to the woods, hunts up the cattle, finds and brings home some " bleen," which she mixes in water, and then washes her floor, on her hands and knees, with this paste.

It prevents the floor from cracking, and forms a crust on it that keeps insects from coming in at night and biting the people while they are asleep on the floor. It cleans the floor, and gives the house the appearance of having had a general straightening up. It is one of the offensive things in African housekeeping, and yet it seems to be necessary to the health and comfort of the household.

Some of the men who have been to sea and have seen European houses come home and build houses with mud walls and with windows. They procure old hinges with which to hang the door—the front door, at least, if they do not have hinges enough to hang the others.

Some of them say, "I no fit to live in them umberella house this time." They have more advanced ideas. So they build a long house instead of a round one, and divide it into two parts, making one half a bedroom and the other the kitchen. When a man builds this kind of house he scorns to sleep on the floor, and makes himself a bedstead—the rudest kind imaginable, but it keeps him off the floor, and he congratulates himself that he has taken one step toward " white man's fashion."

This is the desire of the people in general; and as they become enlightened they will replace their rude huts with respectable houses, and the whole land will testify that the " true Light" has shined upon them.

One of the greatest obstructions in the way of the Gospel in Africa is the rum traffic carried on by the European nations. A few years ago this traffic was not to be compared with what it is to-day. It is not long since one bottle of gin would satisfy all the people in a town; they used to take a spoon to drink it out of. But now when rum comes into town— not by the bottle, but by the barrel—I have seen men stand around it, with brass kettles, tin buckets, iron pots, and tin cans, contending to see who could get the most, and then end-ing up in a fight. The little children stood around sipping the last drop out of the dish father or mother had emptied. Many of the older people think it a good piece of fun to get a child drunk.

During the year 1894 two trading ships were wrecked within twenty miles of Garraway; and, as they were heavily loaded with rum, it was a great curse to us, as well as to the other tribes on the coast. One poor man who fell a victim to the first wreck was a devil-doctor. The people said that this kind of "red rum" must have water put into it before they could drink it. I think it was brandy. It came in a large barrel, which would hold at least forty-five gallons. This man, Kiew, who was a heavy drinker before, bought five gallons on Saturday and drank of it freely. In the evening when he went to cast his fishing net he had a bottle with him. I saw him, just before he went out to fish, getting his net ready.

On Sunday morning he was taken suddenly ill, and felt at once that it was death. He called his oldest son, Bauboo, and said, "My son, I am sick, and I shall die now. I am very sorry to leave you at your age—a young man not married—and all my little children. I am very sorry to-day to have to tell you that I shall have to leave you, but I can't get better."

His family being alarmed, his brother carried him into the other town and hid him away in a small house. They often do this with their sick, believing that some witch is the cause of the sickness, and that when the witch cannot find them the spell will be broken and they will get better. They gave him their country medicines, but he grew worse.

On Monday morning, as I was going around the town making calls, I came to his brother's place. The brother said to me, "I want you to come and see a man who is sick. I went with him, and when we came to the house he opened the door, and there was Kiew with his back up against the wall by a fire, with a brass kettle by his side. I said, "Kiew, is this you?" for I did not know he was sick.

"Yes, teacher," replied the dying man, "I am very sick. Can't you give me some medicine?"

He was panting for breath, and every few minutes hung his head over the brass kettle, while the corruption ran out of his mouth.

I asked his brother, Yaway, if they had done anything for him, and he said, "O yes, we have given him medicine, but it does not do him any good. Haven't you any good medicine?"

His son Boulow sat at the door, and I told him that we must do something quickly, for his father was very sick. So I sent him to the mission to my sister to fetch some medicine. He soon returned; and I gave Kiew the medicine. Meantime, we had taken him outside, spread a mat on the ground, and laid him upon it. He lay quietly for about an hour and a half, and then began to vomit. I sent his son for more medicine, and some breakfast for myself. He went in great haste, for he was very much alarmed about his father.

Kiew asked for water, which we gave him. I went into an adjoining house, and before I came back heard some women who were watching him call out, "Kiew danna?" ("What is the matter?") I rushed back and found his eyes set. I bathed him with cold water. The people tried to stand him on his feet, and called out to him in the attempt to arrest his attention; but he was gone. They ran for gunpowder and blew some up his nose, but there was no sign of life.

His wives and children came and threw themselves on the ground, screaming and crying and clinging to their dead husband and father. The people, in terror, ran every way, crying, "Murder! murder!" Soon a crowd of people gathered in great fright, for few knew that Kiew was ill. They beat the war drum and blew the war horn to call the people from the farms and the bush. Such excitement and confusion I had not seen among our people since the war.

I could do no more. The man was dead, and the people were excited; so I left them and went home. I knew that my sister would be wondering the reason for all the tumult.

In the afternoon she and I went to the town. I said to one of the men, "Rum killed Kiew." He clasped my hand and said, "True, true, it be rum kill him." We visited many of the people. Some were serious, but some were still drinking.

We came to where the body lay. While we were talking a man said, "After you went back this morning Kiew swell up so big we don't know what to do, so we took him out behind the town among the bushes and rolled and squeezed him, and all that stuff came out of his mouth and nose, just like when you open a rum barrel."

Unspeakable corruption set in before they could get him buried. Four men carried him very gently and put him in the grave.

Who can believe that such a body will be raised glorified, to live with our risen Lord in the skies? Surely, when the Judge shall open the book of remembrance and read the details of such a life as this, it cannot receive the "Well done, thou good and faithful servant: enter thou into the joy of thy Lord." Of all the black records of unfaithfulness, surely none can be blacker than the drunkard's. He has been unfaithful to wife, children, friends, neighbors, society, country, himself, and most of all to God.

Some people say, "O, in speaking of rum they always color everything so high. There is no moderation. And then, when they get hold of an extreme case, they cannot stop at telling the truth about it; they must go on and color it up, until you would think it was dangerous to look at a bottle or a barrel if it had rum inside."

But there are no words in the English or any other language that will express the reality of it. When we have said all that our imagination can conceive we have but commenced to tell about it. No coloring has been found in this moderate world vivid enough, nor can the human mind depict a scene that can compare with the penalty entailed by drink.

O Lord, how long shall this devil go to and fro in the earth and walk up and down in it? Well may the Church of God lift up her hands in holy horror and pray, "O Lord, send us deliverance from this demon rum!"

CHAPTER XVI.

A REVIVAL.

The Children's Talk.—The Coming of the Blessing.—Notes from a Journal.—Bestman and Daniel.—"The Big Devil.' —"The Power of God."—"The Sky Coming Down."— Garraway After Seven Years.—Samuel's Letter.—Africa for Christ !

ONE evening we sat on the veranda in the beautiful moonlight of Africa; and the children were talking about the stars and the sky. They commenced by telling the story I have already referred to—how the moon became cold, while the sun is still hot.

They told me, besides, about a fish that the people say once saved a man. They say it was a flying fish. This I believe to be their version of the story of Jonah. There are now three men living in Garraway who will not eat the flying fish. I know them all personally. They say that the man saved by the fish belonged to their family, and in honor of this friendly act to them they will not eat the fish.

The children said that when God made man he made a white man and woman and a black man and woman. He set a table, and at one end put two plates, with knives, forks, spoons, bread, butter, tea, and all kinds of "American food," while at the other end he put one large bowl of palm butter and rice, without any spoons. Then he called them to eat. The white man and woman took the place with the bread, butter, tea, etc., and ate with the knives, forks, and spoons; and the black man and woman took the place with the palm butter and rice and ate with their hands. This was their own choice; and so, because the black man did not take the American victuals, God had made them all fools. Both white and black people might have had the good food; but the black people chose the palm butter and rice, and thus the curse fell on them. The first black people "did them bad," and so they will never have the good things that the white people have. This is their version of the fall of man, but the story has been handed down orally until you can hardly recognize it.

They then repeated their strange story of the last day, which they say their fathers received from the first people. The sea gulls are drinking the oceans dry, the sandpipers counting the sand on the beach, and the woodpeckers cutting down the trees. They will all finish on the same day, the sky will then come down, and then this world will be destroyed.

They told me also of a story they have of God's Son who came into the world. They say he knew everything.

This so impressed me with the fact that these people are responsible to-day for all they do that it threw new light on all my work. Garraway seemed like a new place to me after this; for I had been telling them all these things, thinking they knew nothing about them. And now to learn that they knew and believed all these traditions, so like the Scripture records, gave me a groundwork to begin upon. So far I had not got much hold on them. I felt now that the fact that their fathers had told them before would give me a great hold on them.

"Everything is quiet to-day," I wrote in my journal next day, "and we have school as usual; but the thought of what the children told me makes everything seem different, and I cannot help believing that a new time has come."

After supper the children all took their books and went to study, and I lay down to rest. But the conviction came forcibly to me that I ought to have a religious meeting with the children. Accordingly I told them all to put away their books for the night; and then I explained to them what it was to be saved, or converted, and told them that Jesus wanted to take all the devil out of them and come and live in their hearts himself. I told them that we were going to study about it, that next night we were going to have a penitent bench, and that any one of them who made up his mind to be saved ought to come and be saved, for Jesus had been waiting a long time to save them, and if they were willing he would save them at once.

All next day we felt the presence of the Spirit, though little was said. The children each learned a new verse, and considered the matter. We did not tell those living in "Zion" (our Christian town) that we were going to have a meeting, but the children told the Zion children at school; and in the evening after we had commenced the meeting the Zion children came.

I gave the invitation for any who wanted to be saved to come forward. I told them I did not mean anyone who wanted to pray, for we all prayed, but that God wanted to do something new for them—something they had not yet experienced. (I had already one boy who had received this experience of the new birth the previous March, had lived for God ever since, had the assurance of his acceptance, and had testified to it.)

We all knelt at the bench, and they all prayed at once. George, one of the older boys, was very much troubled, and soon laid all down before God, and it was not long till he knew that he was a free boy and that the burden was gone. O, how he shouted the praises of God! He felt so free that he threw up his arms many times and asked God to take him to heaven at once. I shall never, never forget the night when George was saved.

Before school the following morning the children had a meeting to pray God to save them. The girls went up stairs, and the boys to the schoolhouse. I was in my room, and thought I would let them be alone and get their eyes on God, for I did not want to have them look to me.

The Zion men came to school, and, finding the boys having a prayer meeting, joined them. They were all so much in earnest that they forgot when their half hour was up, and when I rang the bell for school they did not hear. After a time I went to the schoolhouse and found them all on their knees. George had told what a wonderful Saviour he had found, and all the rest were anxious to find him too. When they rose from their knees I asked them if they were ready to have school, and they said yes.

This being our regular prayer meeting night, we all met at the close of the day. We placed the bench in the middle of the room. I said that if anybody wanted God to take the devil out of his heart and come in and live there he had better get down on his knees before him; and they filled the bench.

We had the old-time Methodist shouting. Surely the Spirit came down from heaven, for there was no one there who knew anything about shouting in meeting or had ever attended a revival and seen people saved. They did not shout because they had heard other people do so. No one there knew what was coming. I myself am not a shouter; but I said a loud " amen " to it all.

Jacob was the first saved ; and he was sweetly saved and testified to it. He fell over the bench and lay so for a time ; but when he had the witness of his salvation he was on his feet shouting the praises of God. Whom the Lord makes free are free indeed. Little Mary and Lizzie were saved also.

The next day we had an early morning meeting, and school as usual. A sweet, quiet spirit pervaded our home, such as we had never had before. At seven in the evening we had meeting again, and God was there to bless and save. All who were not converted knelt at the bench, and four of them were saved—Tom, Matilda, Nathan, and Scott. I felt like hiding out of sight and letting the blessing come down. No tongue can tell the joy that filled my heart when I saw those saved for whom I had labored and lived for four long years.

My journal is full on the work of these days:

"*Friday, January* 20.—I have felt that we ought to be quiet, and not do anything that might seem like indifference and grieve the Holy Spirit; for I can just feel that he is hovering around us, ready to enter the willing heart.

"I have never seen the devil try any person as he has our Charles; it does seem as if the devil makes him laugh at everything. He has seemed unable to contain himself until to-day; however, all this day he has been very quiet.

"As the Zion people were not here as soon as we were ready for service, the children all being hoarse from shouting and singing, I said they had better get down and pray. They did, and Charles was the first to pray; and as he did not stop they all commenced, and they all prayed at once. The Zion people came in and brought some town people with them. Before we rose to our feet Charlie was saved. O, he was so very happy, and shouted all kinds of praises to God, and begged everybody to just open his heart and let the dear Saviour come in. It was such a sweet meeting, for we all felt that Jesus was there. Although none but Charlie was saved, we had a good testimony meeting. The town people who had come in were afraid, and could not understand how God's people could be so happy.

"*Saturday, January* 21.—Last evening we said that we should not do any work we could help, but wait on God and look up to him for an especial blessing. The children did the necessary work for Saturday, and two of the larger boys went to the bush for palm nuts, returning about twelve o'clock. After eating their breakfast the children all sat down for prayers. I was tired and lay down in my room to rest.

"As I closed my eyes and looked up to God I could see the Spirit hovering over us, ready to descend in blessing upon us. I could not lie quiet any longer, so got up and went to enjoy the blessing with the children. They were on their knees when the blessing of God came down upon us. Annie was the first to receive Jesus into her heart—she is five years old; next was Solomon, and then Will, my two little boys of six years. I have never heard children shout the praises of God as these three children did,

"At the time that we were praying in the mission the men in Zion felt the Spirit descend, and at once Jacob came up to the mission house. Bestman went into his room in his own house in Zion, but soon felt that he must come to the mission house.

"Daniel was on his farm near by. He heard the shouts of the children and felt that he must come to prayers. He dropped his cutlass and cassada stick, which he was using on the farm, ran to Zion for his Bible, and started for the mission house. When he came to the schoolhouse he felt that he must go in there. So he went in and knelt down to pray for himself—he was not yet saved.

"Bestman, who had been praying alone at home, felt he must come to the mission. Not knowing at all what was going on or that there was anybody there before him, he, too, felt that he must go into the schoolhouse. He went in; and, not knowing Daniel was already there praying, he knelt at the other end of the table from Daniel, and wrestled with God for liberty from the bondage of sin that held him in darkness and distress.

"We were still on our knees at the mission house. Soon Charlie went to the door, and came back and said, 'Teacher, Bestman is saved.' 'How do you know?' I asked. He answered, 'I hear him in the schoolhouse.'

"I went to the door and heard him praising God. The three little children who had just been saved were still on their feet praising God, and I left them there and went to Bestman in the schoolhouse. I found Bestman and Daniel on their knees just entering the kingdom, and wet with perspiration from the struggle to get free. Soon they got through; and O the shouts of victory from those two strong men! They threw their arms around each other, danced round and round the house, and shook everybody's hand, not able to give expression to the joy they felt in being born again—born of God.

"I don't wonder that the people on the day of Pentecost thought that the disciples were full of new wine. I should never be able to make such a demonstration myself; but I would not dare to say it was not of God and just as pleasing to him as my own quiet way. God has many ways of manifesting his power to men.

"A man came in from town just as the two men were rejoicing and telling what God had done for them. He was very much afraid, and felt that the presence of God was with us. He wanted to leave; but I told him that God was here and had come to save sinners, and that he must not go now. He remained until we all left the schoolhouse, and then went to town very much impressed with what had been done.

"After spending some time in testimony and praise to God for his goodness we parted, and the men went home to tell what great things the Lord had done for them.

"In the evening we all met again. Nobody could sing much, so we all prayed. A number of the town people came in. It was the work of those who were converted to go and bring somebody else; so they brought their unsaved friends. We all knelt in prayer, those seeking the Saviour kneeling at the altar. How wonderfully God showed his power among us! All in the room testified, 'Surely the Lord is in this place.'

"The unsaved and those who had come just to see, never having seen anything of the kind before and not knowing that there was such a thing as being born again, were afraid, and went to town and reported that it was the big devil who, they believe, lives on the hill in the big trees, and that he had made us crazy. Four were saved, and there were still more seeking at the altar. We separated at half-past nine, and all went home rejoicing in what God had done for us.

A REVIVAL.

"*Sunday, January* 22.—The Sabbath day. We all went to town to tell the good news and invite sinners to come to Jesus and be saved, taking for our text, 'Humble yourselves in the sight of the Lord, and he shall lift you up.' We had a very interesting meeting, and then went home for our regular morning service at eleven o'clock. After reading the Scriptures, especially some of the promises to those who are seeking Jesus, we knelt in prayer. All who were not saved knelt at the altar.

"One of my big boys, who had been seeking and had one night testified that he believed God had forgiven his sins, had since doubted and was in darkness. When we knelt I began to pray, and he came and put his hands on my shoulders and said, 'Teacher.' I at once took hold of his hands and, without asking him what he wanted, began to pray for him. It was only a few minutes till he fell back with the power of God and began to roll on the floor. He surely did act like a crazy boy, and tore his shirt all to pieces. He rolled out of the door on to the veranda, and fell from there to the ground, a foot below. For about half an hour he kept it up, rolling all around the yard. When the devil was cast out he rose to his feet, but 'walking, and leaping, and praising God' was not sufficient to give expression to the joy he felt in his heart. After a testimony meeting we went home for dinner.

"In the evening we all went out and marched around to three towns, then to Ballie, the king's town. We went inside Sampson's house, and had such a meeting as we had never had in Garraway before. We praised God, testified, and sang the songs of Zion. God's Spirit was with us to convince the people of sin and of his power to save. Captain was saved, and the people in town could but believe in the power of God. Many of them were afraid.

"*Monday, January* 23.—I could not sleep last night; in fact, have not slept nor eaten much for the last week. At the break of day I called all the children, and we went to Tyes town—one of the towns quite near. We did not go alone, for God, our great Leader, was with us, and the people knew we had not come of ourselves. When in town I felt that I should stay there; but the rest seemed ready to go back. So I thought that perhaps it was not of God that we should stay, and so we all went home. I lay down to rest, and the children got breakfast.

"As I lay there I felt that I ought to go to town and stay with the people, but they were having a big dance and drinking rum. One

A REVIVAL.   283

of the traders had been to the Cape and had brought back some rum to treat the women, who were having a big drink. I knew if we had stayed in town in the morning they would not have had their play that day, for I had called at the trader's house, and he, with two other men, had hidden in a small room. I called them all by name, but they refused to answer me or come out of the room. I knelt on the ground at the open door and prayed God to have mercy upon them and help them to turn from the life they were leading.

"The people were afraid, for we commenced just where they were and at what they already believed—that the sky was coming down. We read 2 Peter iii, 8-15. I told them that I had now been here four years, and they saw what I was doing. I was not trading. I was not making money. Since I had been here I had been reading the Bible to them and telling them about God, and that Jesus came and lived and died in this world to save sinners.

"I had taught that when people died they could not live with God in the good world if they did not do his way while they lived here; but that the devil had a very bad place where he and his angels lived, and when people died who did not keep God's law while they were in this world God would not let them come into his home, because they would make palaver (disputes) there and not keep his law. God's home in the sky—they believe that God lives in the sky—would be spoiled by these bad people, just as this world was. So, when God would not let them come in, the devil would just pull them down to hell. They are familiar with the word 'hell,' having learned it as a curseword at sea, and know it is some bad place.

"I said that I was glad that their fathers had told them about the sky's coming down, and that my father had told me; and that when I had learned to read the Book I had read it there myself. The white people believed it, too—anybody that could read the Book could read it for himself. I had come to their country to tell it to them, because I thought they did not know. When Jesus was here in this world he said that when all the people knew of him, 'then shall the end come' (Matt. xxiv, 14).

"'If you do not get ready,' I told them, 'God won't wait long for you. He is waiting now—that is what the Book says. But when God sees you make "hard head"'(an expression much used among them, meaning stubbornness) 'he will cut you down at once—that is what he tells us. He is sparing you a little while, just to see if you will receive him; and if not, you shall be cut down. "Why cumbereth it the ground?"'

"Many came. Others feared to come where we were. A man in the adjoining house came and knelt down, and after a time became so alarmed that he went back into his house and tried to hide behind a box. I went in to find him. He was trembling, and said, 'O yes, I know I ought to leave devil way; I am afraid of God to-day.'

"Soon after he was taken sick, but refused to yield to God. He counted the approval of his neighbors and idols of more value than the blessing God was holding out to him. He died, soon after, as he had lived. It was his last chance. Poor Baffalo! in trying to please his gods, which the devil-doctor had said were angry with him because he would not be a devil-doctor, he joined the devil-doctors and took a few lessons; but God had said, 'Cut it down,' and he died.

"I went to Zion and told the men that I felt I ought to go to town and stay there; that when we were in town the people felt the presence of God; and that when we went back to the mission they felt that we were gone and the devil had charge again. After supper I told the children to get my cot ready, for I believed God wanted me to stay in town.

"So, we started for town, carrying the bed with us. We had a good meeting, keeping this one thing before the people—that the sky was coming down, and we had come to tell them that God said it, and he was not a man, that he should lie. They should believe it and come to Jesus, and he would take the devil out of them, who did not live in the bushes, as some of them say, but in their hearts. Unless they got him out now where would they go when the sky came down? With the devil in the fire in hell—no place else!

"I stood at Sampson's place and called out the names of all the chiefs in the town, and told them we had come to beg them to believe in God, not the devil; to trust in Jesus, not the devil, and be ready; for true, true, the sky was coming down, and I did not know what day, and God said nobody should know but himself. The only thing for us to do was to get ready, for it would come 'like a thief in the night.'

"We said we had come to stay, and if they would not let us sleep in their houses we would sleep on the ground. I consulted the converts. They said, 'Yes, and if need be we will die for the souls of our friends. We have come to stay.' So I said that if they would not give us anything to eat I would give my life for them, and they could carry my body to Zion and bury it there. 'But don't,' I said, 'let the grass grow over me; for, living or dying, I beg of you to be saved by the blood, for there is no other way to God's country.'

"I dismissed the meeting and said, 'Now go to bed and sleep; but if the sky comes down to-night what will you do?' They refused to go away, so I said, 'Well, you must come here and kneel down and beg God to save you.' A great many came. We prayed for the presence of the Spirit to show the need of a Saviour."

O, the darkness of the heathen mind, all blinded with the superstitions of years, so incapable of comprehending the things of God at first, until these obstructions have moved out of the way! They say, " My father told me to wear these charms, worship these gods " —or, rather, make offerings to them, for the African is not a worshiper in the sense that we use the word " worship." He makes offerings to appease the wrath of the dead and of the evil spirits. If he does not attend to these duties, he believes that any calamity that may come to him is the result of his neglect, or of the wrath of some witch man or woman.

So, in keeping the law of his fathers he has

a certain sort of peace. Yet God in his mercy to man has left him "without excuse." He has the law of God written on his heart, and, although he has "changed the truth of God into a lie," yet the original stamp remains, and when you get down to it his heart responds, and he can hear a voice within him saying, "This is the way, walk ye in it."

The journal of this day continues:

"It was growing late, and Sampson had gone. He was afraid, and did not know what to do. He was under conviction, and had been on his knees praying, but, fearing he might get saved and become a Christian, he had left and was not to be found. We took possession of his largest house. Finding mats tied up to the ceiling, we took them down and made our beds, the children and myself, fourteen in all.

"As no person put in an appearance we lay down to sleep, after shutting the doors. When all was quiet, Sampson came and called out, 'Teacher, did you get a bed?' I said, 'Yes; where are you going to sleep?' 'O, I'll find a place,' he answered."

No amount of "excitement" could have put me through what I went through that month. But I believe God does not always choose persons especially gifted, but those who will deliver the message he gives. How often have you thought you should speak to some person about his soul, yet, because it would seem out of place or you would seem peculiar, you have not done so? "Be not conformed to this world." What does that mean but that we are not to be as they are or do as they do? "A peculiar people." O, how we shrink from being peculiar! How we rob God of his glory and retard the wheels of the Gospel chariot by not delivering the message given by the King! Let us fear to disobey our God, though all the people think us peculiar or crazy and fail not to report their opinion of us.

The father of one of our girls from the interior heard that I had gone crazy and had seen the devil, and came down in great haste one morning to see what was to be done with his daughter. When he came he at once told me what had brought him, and said, "O, I be very glad to see you better; we hear news in our town that you be sick bad."

"No, no," I said, "I am not sick, but the Garraway people told me some big news. Do you know the sky is coming down?"

He answered, "I have been hear about that when I was a small boy, and it make me afraid;

but this time I think the sky is no fit to come down no more."

After some conversation on the traditions and customs of the people, referring especially to their custom of firing guns, beating drums, and blowing their war horns, in time of a thunderstorm, with the hope that the great noise may reach God's ear and he be persuaded to have mercy on them and not let the sky down for the present, he said, "You talk true; we all do that." After I had read some passages from the Word to him, he said, "Them book talk true; we know this world can finish."

He is one of many that have the truth of God written on their hearts. God has given us the work of lifting up Jesus to a perishing world, and the heathen feel their need of him as other sinners do. We had those among us who, when we came, were in sin and caring for none of God's ways; but, because we told them of a Saviour and pointed them to him who alone can save, they have been persuaded to turn to him for salvation, and are now rejoicing in his love.

When we went to Garraway, six and a half years ago, there was no knowledge of the Sabbath, no religious services, no school, not one person that could spell or write his own name. Now the people know that the seventh day is the Sabbath of the Lord our God, to be kept holy.

We have a church organization, although not a church building. The services are held in the mission house. We have thirty-two members. Every Sabbath morning we have open-air meetings in two towns. At eleven o'clock we have the regular morning service, followed by a fellowship meeting at the close. At four o'clock we have Sabbath school. Wednesday evening we have our regular prayer meeting; and Friday evening the children have their meeting.

On a moonlight night it is a very common thing for some of our members to march into the town, sing up a crowd of the people, interest them by telling them of God and eternal life, and urge them to accept salvation. The native children in the towns sometimes gather together and go from town to town singing Gospel songs.

In our Christian town, Zion, our people gather at the close of the day in somebody's house or yard, and have worship together before retiring. These gatherings are often rather prayer meetings than family worship, as they sing, recite Bible verses, and sometimes have an experience meeting. And they have an experience to tell.

I give here a letter I received from one of our boys when I was away from home. He has been in the school four and a half years. He knew nothing of books, and but few English words, when he came:

"GARRAWAY, *September* 17, 1895.
"MY DEAR TEACHER:
"I received your letter. We all are well. We have been in the interior and cleaned the coffee there, and have had a good time. I wish you were here to eat some of the palm butter and rice.

"Hallelujah! We are doing all we can to stir this country for God. The people are hungry for the real Gospel. We are expecting to see done that shall astonish men and devils and glorify our God forever. We praise the Lord for those he has saved, and ask for more and more. O hallelujah!

"These are the very best days of all my life —days of sharp contest with the foe and complete and sweeping victory. It seems to me that the sunlight of heaven never shone so bright on my soul as now. The cross never seemed so precious, the way so bright, and our lovely Jesus so near and dear. Bless his name! Fellow-workers, I am with you to stand by this clean way until I lay down the cross and receive the crown. Amen! Let us be true to the trust he has left us, and never shrink or falter, gladly bearing the cross.

"Your loving boy,
"SAMUEL JAMES MONY."

This letter of Samuel's shows what has been done for him in our day school. We have upon an average twelve scholars, and teach five days in the week.

Many of our people are very proud of what they have accomplished; and they have reason to be. The mission has done for them what nothing else has ever done; and some of the old heathen men, who never intend to become Christians themselves, will encourage the young men and say, "You must do this new way; our old fashion never fit to do us better." And when they see their sons learning to read and write and dressed like civilized people they feel that brighter days have come to them, and hope that they may rise from the ignorance of the past to enjoy the advantages and privileges that civilization and Christianity bring to every nation where they are received. The natives know a good thing when they see it, and are quite convinced that the mission has done them more good than anything they could do for themselves.

Africa is the land to which all eyes are being turned in these days. It offers to the explorer the grandest lakes, rivers, and forests the world can give; to the hunter, all kinds of game; to the miner, untold wealth. But to the missionary it is, in these last days, the land where jewels bright and sparkling are to be found, that shall shine through all eternity as stars in the crown of Him who died to save the lost.

Fellow-missionaries, let us rejoice, even if things may look dark before us at times. I have seen very dark days in Garraway, and know I shall see them again; but God lives, and has given us many blessings along the way. Sometimes it looks as if the people will not accept the Gospel; but when the darkness is past, if we have trusted God through it, we can see the rays of light on the other side. Let us praise our Almighty God and exalt his name together. The showers are coming; these are only the first drops we feel now to tell us the season has come.

Some people very skeptically ask, " Do you think you are doing any good? Have you any idea that the native people will accept Christianity or be benefited by your going to them?" O yes, if I believe there is a God, whose word we read, I must believe that it is doing good to obey his voice. Even in my short day I have seen his word fulfilled in so many ways that I must believe it all.

The little stone that Nebuchadnezzar saw, that struck his powerful image and sent it like chaff before the wind, is this Jesus that we preach. Let us obey his every command, heeding not how dark it looks to human eyes if only we have Jesus on our side.

> "We're a band that shall conquer the foe,
> If we fight in the strength of the King;
> With the sword of the Spirit we know
> We shall sinners to Calvary bring."

THE END.

www.ingramcontent.com/pod-product-compliance
Lightning Source LLC
Chambersburg PA
CBHW032058220426
43664CB00008B/1053